# THE ETERN

*A Kaleidoscope of Divine Inspired Thought Sparks*

By
ROBERT ERNST DICKHOFF, Ph. D.D.D.

BOSTON
BRUCE HUMPHRIES, INC.
PUBLISHERS

Copyright, 1947, by
BRUCE HUMPHRIES, INC.

Printed in the United States of America

DORDJELUTRU
Mountain God of Minya Konka, Tibet
*From a painting by Robert Ernst Dickhoff*

*To the fearless, mental pioneers who beheld the Cosmic Image of Divine Heritage within their Souls this book is dedicated, as a constant reminder of what earthlings should not be, of what they are, and of what they are to be.*

# CHANT OF FAITH

*OMnipresent Lord on high,*
*Ruler of the earth and sky,*
*Bless us creatures far and wide*
*Such as live and die for right.*

*OMniscience is thy name,*
*Which puts wizards here to shame.*
*Let their magic come to naught*
*And the evils they have taught.*

*OMnipotent are thy charms,*
*Aid and comfort in Thy arms.*
*Find your servants — which become*
*Leading teachers of the OM.*

# FOREWORD

THIS book is a collection of essays on various subjects. Because of its inspired origin and the message hidden within its lines, it will hold the interest of its readers. The contents took many years to write, but its worth will be realized, for it not only deals with events of the past and the present, but it reaches far out into the future. It is a book easily understood, due to its plain wording; thus even the most humble of humans may benefit by the mass of spiritual truths presented, and may often experience a sensation of awe, once the arcane wisdom gathered becomes within the reach of understanding. The correct penetration of the psychic realm has been reached by few mortals in a manner to enable them to instruct others in their own lifetime. All my impressions are of a truly occult nature, as one that sees with an inner eye the workings of a living cosmos and, free from superstition, admires the hidden forces that motivate all creation.

ROBERT ERNST DICKHOFF

*Most Rev. Red Lama*

## CONTENTS

| | |
|---|---|
| *Maitreya The World Teacher* | 13 |
| *The Most High God Asks of You* | 16 |
| *What Price Civilization?* | 18 |
| *Thought . . . The Ruler of the Universe* | 22 |
| *Suicide* | 26 |
| *Sterilization* | 29 |
| *The Germ of Life—A Parasite, Blessing or Curse?* | 33 |
| *Behold the Valley of Thy Soul* | 38 |
| *Clairvoyant — Prophesy* | 42 |
| *God Is . . .* | 48 |
| *Atlantis* | 55 |
| *Mental Dynamite: Words* | 61 |
| *Meditation* | 65 |
| *Concentration* | 67 |
| *Sound and Light* | 70 |
| *Man — The Super Animal* | 74 |
| *Pioneers of Tomorrow* | 79 |
| *Fear — The Invisible Ruler* | 84 |
| *Live According to Nature and Be Healthy!* | 88 |
| *Symbolic Sun Worship* | 92 |
| *Atomic Attraction, Concentration, and Adjustment* | 96 |
| *Spiritual Thought Renaissance* | 98 |
| *Spiritual Concept and Materialization* | 100 |
| *Symbolic Language* | 108 |
| *Novus Ordo Seclorum* | 111 |
| *The Children of "Heaven and Earth"* | 116 |
| *"So Be It Unto You"* | 121 |
| *Sayings of Red Lama* | 123 |
| *The Mystic Talisman* | 128 |

# THE ETERNAL FOUNTAIN

# MAITREYA THE WORLD TEACHER

*Buddha's Prophesy Concerning Maitreya*

And the Blessed One said to Ananda: "I am not the first Buddha who has come to the earth nor shall I be the last. In due time another Buddha will arise in the world, a Holy One, a supremely enlightened One, endowed with wisdom embracing the universe, an incomparable leader of men, a ruler of devas and mortals. He will reveal to you the same eternal truths which I have taught you. He will establish his law, glorious in its origin, glorious at the climax and glorious at the goal in the spiritual and in the letter. He will proclaim a righteous life wholly perfect and pure, such as I now proclaim. His disciples will number many thousands, while mine number hundreds."

Ananda said: "How shall we know him?" — The Blessed One said: "He will be known as Maitreya, the Lord of Compassion and World Teacher."

The Advent of Maitreya according to "Digha Nikaya" dialogue 26, quoting the words of Buddha Guatama, concerning a message of his disciples, "Monks, in the days when men will live 800 years, there will arise in the world a Buddha named Maitreya, the Compassionate One, a supremely Enlightened One, endowed with wisdom in conduct, auspicious, knowing the universe, an incomparable charioteer of men who are tamed, a master of angels and mortals, a blessed Buddha, even as I have now arisen in the world, a

Buddha with these same qualities endowed. What he has realized by his own superior knowledge, he will publish to the universe with its angels, its friends, its archangels and to the race of philosophers, brahmins, princes and people, even as I now having all this knowledge, do publish the same unto the same. He will proclaim a righteous life, wholly perfect and pure, even as I now preach my philosophy and a like Life do proclaim. He will keep a society of monks numbering many thousands, even as I now keep up a society of monks numbering many hundreds."

### *Prophesy of Guru Avananda Concerning Maitreya*

"First will begin an unprecedented war of all nations. Afterwards brother shall rise against brother — oceans of blood shall flow. People shall forget the meaning of the word. But then shall the teacher appear and in all the corners of the world shall be heard the true teaching. To the word of truth shall the people be drawn, but such as are filled with darkness and ignorance shall set obstacles. As a diamond glows on the Tower of Shambala, one stone on his ring is worth more than all the treasures of the world. Many of the warriors of the teaching of truth are already reincarnated. Only a few years shall lapse before every one shall hear the mighty steps of the Lord of the New Era — Maitreya. The banner of Shambala (Spiritual Communicant) shall encircle the central lands of the Blessed One. Those who accept him shall rejoice and those who deny him shall tremble — and the warriors shall march under the banner of Maitreya."

Maitreya as seen by the Lord Maha Chohan Kwang Hsih, H. H. the Prince Om Cherenzi-Lind now in

Habana, Cuba. Quoting from his Wesak Message of 1934: "The Lord Maitreya is not yet fully manifested and let it be understood, will never be a person, although the sense-deluded mystics and the anthropomorphists of religion will give him a human form, with whiskers and all. The Lord Maitreya will only be a cosmic or universal aim and urge, endeavor and value. principle and realization — not a man, a messiah or a divinity."

### Signs of MAITREYA

"In the Era of MAITREYA, the World Teacher — NOW — flowers shall bloom in profusion and out of season and the Woman of the specie called Mankind shall wear them, besides clothes of contrasting, but harmonious colors. The music and dances of South America shall become predominant. The country now named Ecuador, S. A., will become the Spiritual Center, the Tibet of the West, after Maitreya the World Teacher has established himself over all the Earth under the Banner of Maitreya —which is Truth and Justice for *all* Earthlings."

OM MANI PADME HUM
RED LAMA — (SUNGMA-ORACLE)
ROBERT ERNST DICKHOFF, PH. D. D.D.

"In the Era of the Lord Maitreya may Truth and Justice reign supreme."

OM MANI PADME HUM
Oh, Thou Jewel in the Lotus.

MOST REV. *RED LAMA*

## THE MOST HIGH GOD ASKS OF YOU

WHEN you pray, do so in all silence, serenity, and sincerity of Spirit. For I am free Spirit and cannot be bribed into your houses of worship of the one or the other, filled with priests of earth not ordained by me. Your noisy, worldly, showy prayer is unto me like a waterfall, monotonous and without meaning, too loud to be heard even by mine ears. By the standards of men you will have your reward, in praise, ridicule, or abuse; but as for me, give your praise in silence and away from prying eyes of men. Thus I will lift your Soul above the highest edifice of man, even beyond the highest mountains of earth will I lift your Spirit, to have your communion with me.

From time to time I have reminded men that I wish for living temples within their living bodies, rather than man-made houses of worship. I, who have sent a "sword" upon earth for all to see, I who have ordered the scourging of all mankind, giving no protection, order the leveling of your earth temples, churches, mosques, and pagodas which, being but mortar, stone, and clay, and unlike yourselves, cannot reach me. For truly I say unto you, Ants have surpassed man in this. Build ye rather, an edifice within the consciousness of your own Soul, a living temple into which I may enter and be glorified, and where I may bring to you the fulfillment of all desires and wishes within reason.

Does man think in his foolish mind that with his many temples of earth he can surpass mountains, even the hills I gave unto him? Does he honestly think that by ringing bells and by burning incense and candles he may work out his own salvation and that of others more successfully than by humbly seeking my presence within the sanctuary of his home, away from men, but in all sincerity of Spirit? If he does, he is a fool, for in spite of all his churches, he will still have strife and wars and man-made miseries, because his heart and Soul does not truly worship me. His eyes are blinded by a material world and its ways, because by nature he is evil and of earth.

It is, however, given to all to work out their salvation here on earth. Those who set aside moments for meditation on the construction of their own living temples I will instruct, and will divinely protect the portals of such edifices; for I am Spirit, and it is through the power of my Word that all things have their being. I AM the MOST HIGH GOD, who jealously guards truth, and who speaks, through my servants and oracles on earth, of matters pertaining to truth and the laws of nature. For this I exact a price — a strict obedience by all— and I divinely bless those who cleanse their temples in privacy and become a light to the world, an inspiration to follow. Be ye, therefore, transformed into living temples, have a happiness about you which is not of this world, a thankful Spirit at all times; for you are children of flame that will not destroy or consume, but will illumine the life of all earth dwellers and, will heat the temple of Spirit, which shall live within you forever.

## WHAT PRICE CIVILIZATION?

How can there be civilization as long as the rich live on the poor, one religion calls another false, one political party fights another, one race discriminates against another, one nation tries to wipe out weaker nations, using any effective means including war? As long as science uses its might in peace time to invent and to manufacture labor-saving machinery, which causes unemployment and longer bread lines, which benefits only a few and is a curse to millions; as long as the same science turns out deadly chemicals and gases during war time — also for the benefit of a few and aimed at the extinction of millions — there can be no civilization as such. Anyone who praises or introduces such progressive "medicine" for humanity must be a lunatic. We do not live, as did the cannibals of ancient time, by feeding on human flesh and blood, but is not our system of "civilization" worse when judged by its slow, murdering accomplishments through hunger, misery, unemployment, and incurable disease?

In all these things the super animal, man, cannot boast, for such achievements will in the long run cripple humanity to such an extent that extinction of its species is inevitable and only a matter of time. However, I am sure that before the human race lets itself be butchered in order to please our present overlords and financiers, the creatures called men will unite to get rid of these parasites even if they have to go back to the cave age and so-called barbarism and begin all over again. Our present state of civilization, when compared with the life of uncivilized, primitive tribes, is low in its ratio of happiness. The "back-to-nature" movement will become a fact as soon as modern science is through wasting its time, money, and labor on experiments and inventions benefiting only a wealthy few and exploiting or destroying millions of their fellow creatures.

Primitive barbarians, as we call them, live more content in their own beliefs and surroundings than when molested with white man's civilization. This has been proven on numerous occasions (Indians, Eskimos, South Sea Islanders). The white man first introduced religion, then the evil influence of alcohol, in order to force recognition of his civilization and to sell products from "civilized" countries in the territory of the natives. The policy "eat my stuff or die" is well made use of. Not out of pure love for our "brothers," continents are being explored, and when found inhabited the process of civilizing is begun. The word civilization is the prostitute of cunning adventurers, business men, and financiers who regard only their own benefit. It is not out of pure love for our neighbors that missionaries are being sent into far-off lands. The priest must lay the foundation and "fertilize" the "barbarian" mind to the point where any government which wishes to claim the continent or island finds it easy to enforce its own type of law and order among the savages in the newly-conquered land. Should the natives resist the new law — well, there is but one way to enforce civilization — by the sword or similar means powerful enough to enforce obedience.

Back of all this is the scheming monster, the corrupt money-god, which uses as a mask for its actions the phrase, "in the name of civilization and humanity." If the financiers of the world did not profit by the work and the methods of their prostitute, "civilization," they would not give a damn for all the far-off islands and their natives. Cheap labor, new markets, immense profits, are the reasons for civilization. When there is difficulty in securing new markets, when one civilized nation becomes too active in the eyes of other civilized nations, then there will be rivalry, conflict, and finally a bloody war, in order to determine just who is the true carrier of this thing called civilization.

Millions of men, women, and children have been sacrificed on the altar of demon "civilization." Millions will still suffer on account of this "great age of civilization." The natives of inner Australia and Africa do not know the evil behind the white man's charming promises. They do not need Fords to travel in. They do not need to take the risk of being run down by motor vehicles of any kind. In the United States of America there have been about thirty thousand persons killed and wounded by motor cars in a single year. Is the possession of automobiles progress? How can it be, when thirty thousand humans are injured or slaughtered in order to assure profits for the automobile manufacturer? Permitting, or rather demanding, automobiles causes this horrible sacrifice on the altar of modern civilization. On the other hand, missionaries, politicians, and others, raise the devil when one of their subjects, in being too zealous preaching the doctrine of wonderful, civilized achievements in his homeland, wanders off into another tribe and ends up in the stewpot! It seems to me that those natives are exactly right when they prefer their stew-pots to the evil of the more cultivated existence which the white man wishes to promote and, later on, to force upon them. The time may not be far off when all humans will realize the futility of so-called civilization and will return to stew-pots filled with missionaries, crooked politicians, grafters, financiers, and other aboriginals. It certainly would be one unfailing method by which to eliminate the parasites which have exploited humanity since the dawn of creation.

# THOUGHT...THE RULER OF THE UNIVERSE

*Son of Man, when thou doth reacheth a Most High Mountain,*
*Keep thy Silence, for thou art on Holy Ground,*
*Lest the gods find thy babbling most annoying and*
*Bring to thee an avalanche of swift Destruction.*

WHAT is thought? Has it ever occurred to you that we are all living radio sets, being both receiver and broadcaster? Thought waves of unknown frequency find their way into our personal set through our control station, the brain. Thought, a bodyless form of creation, travels at unlimited speed toward our personal radio set; and time, which may be compared to the dial, takes care of the reception. If your receiver is tuned in at the right time, you will receive messages beyond any limit, far-advanced ideas — some within, and some beyond reason or understanding. For the time being, you will be influenced by, and figuratively obliged to obey, the trends of those messages.

Religious people insist that thought waves are of divine origin; they call them a "God-send," and believe them to be omnipotent. What do we actually know about the origin of magnetism, electricity, the cosmic ray, or radio waves — even though we recognize them, take them for granted, and make use of their power? Without thought, we would not even try to understand these forces which now seem beyond reasoning. Thought comes to us as a gift, and we pass it on to others when we feel it will be of use to them. Thought waves live forever on this planet, on neighboring planets, and throughout the universe. If you receive thought waves or messages of, let us say, a political character, which only a comparatively few contemporaries have received and understood, you will soon be called a prophet. And in this case, generations may pass before enough thought messages have been poured into the brain, or power house, of the average human to bring about the same general opinion as that which you picked up prematurely, ages before. This should be sufficient evidence that the Spirit or thought (call it what you may) lives forever — if not in your mind, then in the minds of others throughout all time.

In your brain, thought will do the fertilizing work which will accompany you throughout life, but leave you instantly when you die, and wander on until some other personal "radio set" is capable of receiving that same thought. Time knowing no limit; likewise thought cannot be measured. Both are beyond comprehension, neither having birth or death or limitations of space or speed. Thought, the ruler of the universe, may travel in a split second to the farthest constellations or nebulae. Your personal thought may reach Mars, Venus, or any other planet in our solar system in speed dimensions beyond comparison. Being limited to but human reasoning power, we may not be able to receive and to understand the thought of our brothers on these planets. What we need is a transformer for universal thought reception; but at present death is the only substitute we know for that transformer — it releases personal thought from its human casing and allows it to travel wherever it wishes to go.

Religious people insist that their Spirit, Soul, or thought, will go to Heaven after death. I prefer to assume that, while it does actually leave the body, it merely travels toward other planets, with unchecked speed, but without definite destination. It travels indefinitely until somewhere, some being, form, or creature with intelligence, has its personal radio so tuned as to receive that thought or Spirit which no longer can rule in the body of the deceased. I am convinced that, if my last wish or thought is to become an inhabitant of Mars, and if I am willing to adopt the shape of any intelligent being, as soon as my mortal shell dies, my Spirit or thought will undertake the journey to Mars at lightning speed until it will be picked up by a Martian who has his mind tuned for a reception of that kind. Who knows whether Martians already rule earthlings, not by rod or by law, but by thought? No one can possibly prove the contrary. So let us assume that Martians are more intelligent than earthlings, having solved the mysteries of thought transmission, and understanding it, let us say, as well as we understand the use of the telephone. Believing this, people would welcome the opportunity which many of us dread, namely death. They would know that after the death of their mortal forms they would be free to travel toward Mars or elsewhere, to lead a new and more pleasant life which conditions and circumstances made impossible in their own world.

Thought, the universal vagabond, after influencing the creature it chose for its temporary home and leaving it at death, drifts on through boundless space, at speed unknown, until it again finds a living radio set to its liking. All this may sound fantastic. Maybe it smacks of a new philosophy or doctrine in which death holds no horror. It does offer a "Heaven" where superstition is an impossibility, where there is no judgment to be afraid of. Where thought is the highest ruler of the universe, judgment would be eliminated; there would be no fanaticism. Freedom of the mind would exist not in mind alone, but would be in practice by all reasoning creatures. The stimulating news of such a future need not drive us into insanity and suicide in an attempt to speed up the journey toward a desired goal. Rather, it would make it far easier to bear our burden through this life in anticipation of a worth while and just reward in the form of thought transplantation beyond space, at one's own free will. Death would be the ferryman, asking nothing in return, but giving the thought, your thought, freedom to leave for unbounded adventure into strange worlds, among strange beings, to live in them with its own fertile power of reasoning.

At a recent congress of scientists a speaker prophesied that soon the human race would be establishing itself in new lands in the sky. A self-sustaining colony that would grow its own food, produce and rear children, is beyond possibility in our present state of advancement on any planet the astronomer knows anything about, with the possible exception of Mars.

# SUICIDE

Is it crime? Is it the way out? Is it a confession of disgust with life, a rebellion against nature's uncanny force which knows not love or hate, which grants no favors, and which gives and then takes life as it pleases? Suicide is not a crime. The individual can do as he pleases with his own body — either prolong the short span of life, or cut it still shorter of his own free will. It is neither a courageous nor a cowardly act. Life, as such, is not worth worrying about, be it long or short. It does not matter much whether a person lives for fifty or a hundred and fifty years. While living may be important to one who has every joy and comfort life can possibly offer, its quick termination may be welcome to one who knows only sorrow and never-ending struggle. The few bright moments during the average lifetime are not sufficient to push aside the ever-growing shadows of misfortune, misery, starvation, and common ailments which must be eliminated if the human race is to survive much longer. We are fighting a losing fight, a struggle not worth while, not worthy even of consideration. Those who realize this true fact but still cling with super-human strength to the last remaining straw must finally let go and sink beneath their hopes, in utter bewilderment, into the wide abyss of deadless time and space.

The ambition of each of us two-legged termites is to shine as brightly as possible while amongst our own kind, always forgetting that, the more energy we use in order to shine, the quicker this energy burns itself out and leaves only the empty shell. No one likes to be pushed aside, to realize his own uselessness, and it is this which often leads to suicide. The straw onto which the individual held becomes too weak to support the hopes and personal desires of its owner. For such individuals suicide is "the way out." Such men defeat nature, since they are one step ahead. But nature is indifferent; it simply is unimportant that so-and-so has stepped more or less quickly over the rim of reasoning into the wide chasm of eternity.

Time, the master clock of the universe, knows neither birth nor death of planets. How much less important are we, then, who, by mere coincident or accident, perform a small task on one of the many planets! We are frightened at the least tremble of the earth, even at thunder. We cover our face when lightning, tornado, or blizzard strikes our neighborhood. We are terror-stricken at the thought of a possible tidal wave. And no one is free of the superstition, inherited through endless generations, that some day, from somewhere, a comet may destroy all of us in a single unit of time. Still we try not to show fear; still we tell each other how important and how brave we are; still we believe that certain individuals must rule over the majority of peoples, and even the moon and the stars are not safe from the mad mind of man in his quest for power. However, our importance here is, in reality, exceedingly limited. There would be none of us, in the first place, without nature's good will. Nature, the creator of everything alive, has wisely ordained that none of its puny creatures may run amuck and create at their own will. Man, no matter how intelligent he deems himself to be, is not able to produce, without the aid of nature, to say nothing of creating a life-sustaining blood corpuscle for animal and human life. We tiny, living earthlings will never be able to understand and to solve mysteries beyond the limit of human reasoning. We have tried in the past, and no doubt many will try in the future; but the only reward nature has in store for such foolish meddlers is failure, insanity, and possible suicide.

Many have gone this road, and many are sure to follow. Suicides caused under such conditions are absolute proof of the complete and inevitable failure which follows humans who tamper with problems not meant for them. Our limited, three-dimensional brains are not fit to tackle such forbidden tasks.

Other suicides are simply personal emergency measures, caused directly by starvation, ill treatment, and neglect, as a result of one or the other system of society. After all, as long as you are master of your own body, it is entirely up to you to decide when to return once more to nature's storehouse — eternity. It does not matter by how many seconds you are cheating nature out of a job, because you are merely remodeling what once was into elements and things that are to be.

## STERILIZATION

One has heard much about sterilization laws. Without doubt, those who oppose it are in the majority. Those who are for it can be found all over the world. It is quite unimportant, whether you are for or against such a law, when you consider the methods used in other countries to attack life itself by an invisible yet more vicious and deadly sterilization. The majority of people give it hardly a thought that during periods of depression — and always among the poor classes — there exists an invisible sterilization on a broad base, forced indirectly upon humans by their leaders. When doles and charity are handed out, people soon lose their morals to the point where they do not consider it worth while to aid in the creation of new life. So this is left to the better-off population, and they create their own peculiar species which they consider "superior."

The younger generation today is skeptical of such schemes, and rightly so. They are healthy, and nature urges them to do what rightfully is their duty. Yet what is not denied to the lower animal — liberty of sex function during mating time — is denied of young people. The fear of having offspring, of untold sorrow and deprivation, stops them in their attempt and throws them into the arms of unlawful, vice-ridden actions, disease, and death. No human law can prevent nature's urge, nor oppress it forever. The dole handed out to fill stomachs temporarily is not meant to fill the mind and Soul of a human being. Thus it certainly cannot banish the natural urge of what is called love, and its ultimate consequences. No leader can tell his people to breed or to stop breeding unless an actual sterilization law has become a fact, and nation wide. Against such a law humans would soon revolt, and would defend their personal happiness to the last ditch. Yet, strange to say, no one else has the courage to speak of the untold misery and horror, mental as well as physical caused by a slow starvation of sex, caused by clever but devilish schemes of a few dishonest politicians, which thus force the minds of their subjects into other than natural channels. People who do not marry out of fear that they will not be able to bring forth children because of lack of the necessities of life, are by no means deprived of their normal sex function. They will soon search and find other outlets to suit their personal demands. Nature must be satisfied, even if abused; and the consequences of abuse are easily understood. Drugs do the rest, when everything else has failed, thus burning the candle at both ends.

Let there be no misconception over the far-reaching results which such invisible sterilization has on the family, as well as on the nation. If deprived for years of the most natural outlet, people will be, in the next generation, unable to breed at all, for lack of understanding and physical strength. A body ridden by vice and drug is hardly capable of reproducing itself; and if it does, the offspring are but horrible reminders of the devilish scheme which indirect sterilization has meant for the broad masses. A race of such imbeciles and morons will soon be under their tombstones. Those guilty of this crime of the century will not escape. They, too, will have dug their graves by greedy, "superior-crazy" selfish desires to outbreed the multitude.

No human has the right to interefere with nature and its supreme laws; only fools attempt such vain and insane tasks. They can change the gold standard and the living standard, but to change the standard of nature is plain suicide. Cattle will breed when the time comes, regardless of famine or of consequences. All other animals live up to the same universal rule, but man— the super animal— tries to get away with something, unharmed. But nature will catch up, and then calamity cannot be avoided. People will not stand being stepped on forever, certainly not when their right to propagate their own species is in danger. When the sexes meet, there must be results; and if that-craving has been stolen by slow, deliberate starving of the body, hell is too good for the sinister schemers who stole it. It is the young generation which suffers most of all. They cannot get married, even if they honestly desire to. There is no work to provide the essentials of living. Even if they have the nerve to go through with it, misery overtakes them all too soon. Those who are employed are shivering in constant fear of losing their jobs, even though these may be but part time affairs. Earnings are so low that they can cover the essentials only scantily, provided there is no newcomer to upset the budget. To live on relief, dole, or charity is dishonoring and demoralizing, and certainly the dole is not large enough to justify the creation of a new life.

Divorces are due to follow, one person blaming the other for the failure and entirely forgetting to mention the real evil of society of "advanced" civilization. The ones which stay single must carry the burden of abnormal taxation, enforcing this invisible steriliza tion; but they continue to suffer for the rest of their miserable lives, by sex starvation in connection with twisted, abnormal abominations. The generation to be born out of such degrading abnormality will certainly do much to bring about a complete and chaotic failure, speeding toward the ruin of a race called humans and its demon rulers. The only remedy is work and more work for all concerned. Honest work must be found — even if people are made to build towers ten times the size, and better in construction and art than the pyramids of the Cheops of ancient Egypt — even if they build tunnels to connect Europe and this continent, inaugurate space travel via spaceships, just so that lifetime work is secured and people begin smiling again, inspired by new ideals and a better morale, so that nature once more will function in accordance and in harmony with its perpetual law.

# THE GERM OF LIFE — A PARASITE, BLESSING, OR CURSE?

FROM the cradle to the grave we are attacked and slowly devoured by almost invisible, yet merciless enemies: germs, spores, microbes, which float in the air, contaminate the water, and grow in the ground. We breathe them, eat them with our food, and swallow them even now as we read or talk. In uncountable millions they become parasites in our systems, feasting on and destroying our very lives. Where they actually come from is immaterial; they are here in spite of everything, and finding fertile soil they grow and multiply at a rate beyond anything imaginable. Even after their victim's death they keep on eating until there is nothing left to consume. The wind and every moving energy furnishes them adequate transportation, and no place is safe, no person immune. While immunization against some diseases is now possible, it has still to be discovered for tuberculosis, influenza, infantile paralysis, sleeping sickness, cancer, syphilis, trichinosis, etc. The ravages of the parasites causing these diseases are enormous; and human beings stand helpless before their tiny destroyers. Small as they are, their numbers win in the endless and unrelenting battle. Life must go on — even if it is the life of the parasite germs.

The universe with all its planets is immeasurable, and its entire expanse seems to offer food and shelter for the little creatures which eventually force their way into our system. Our reproductive system is infested with life-giving germs which provide again new "fleshpots" for our enemies. They seem to be one happy family, and we are but the sacrifice. They enjoy a bacchanal supreme, with our indirect and helpless consent, and eat away our health, happiness, and life itself in a short time. As the kernel or seed of an apple or other fruit is hidden at its center, sometimes protected by an amazing vault of strength, so the living germs or seed of the species is hidden in the human body. Nature made the flesh of the apple appealing to its consumer, so that he would eat the flesh and release the seed; likewise nature made the human body appealing to the opposite sex, the release and fertilization of the living germ depending entirely on time, place, and circumstance. It is not men and women who are finding one another; it is the influence of a power which is paramount in the germ of life and which uses the human body more or less as a house of its choosing, for protection and survival.

We are but the slaves of these living parasites. No one can deny that the urge of sex life has not shaped his entire career into channels not originally planned. The history of mankind tells the story — tribes, nations, civilizations of the past have been annihilated, not merely to satisfy the sex lust of the conqueror, but to fulfill the desire of the life germ, under the spell of which man has been as one under the influence of a stimulating drug. It seems as though these parasites are asking for better bodies to live in — more comfortable and better protected — as though they say, "You must kill if no other means can be found, so that we may live more securely." Men and women are secondary to the life germ. Subconsciously we all know

## The Germ of Life—A Parasite, Blessing or Curse? 35

it, but we hate to admit it. We, the carriers of life seed, like the apple, are soon forgotten when the pretty outside shell is no longer of any use to the germ of life. These seeds have found their way into another storehouse, where they can grow and dominate again. Just as a tree will bear fruit year after year in order that some of its seeds may again come into contact with fertile soil and so reproduce once more, so it is with the reproduction of live germs in the human body — though being of different composition, the method of replanting the seed of life is different. The urge and the results, however, remain the same.

There are infinite numbers of quivering germs ready to be released when they come in contact with the desired environment. These germs live when all else is dead. Their resistance is amazing. They are hampered by neither time, temperature, nor space. Corn which has been entombed for thousands of years, together with the embalmed bodies of Egyptian rulers, were found to bear fruit when they were brought into contact with their element. Meterorites, upon examination under the microscope, showed germs and spores carried from other planets but still alive and clinging to the masses after defying the cold of outer space and the intense heat created by friction, when the meteorites came into contact with our atmosphere. If transplanted into their own element, whatever that might be, who knows what weird forms of vegetation, insect, animal, or even human form they might produce? Man, animal, insect, and all life attributes its existence to the favorable conditions under which the life germs can settle and survive. They do survive floating on the beam of light itself, defying all elements, traveling from planet to planet, teaching man of his insignificance. In solid blocks of ice in the polar regions they are waiting to be released. Time means nothing — they are almost immortal — and they wait patiently for favorable conditions when they may again create new beings, super vegetation, super beasts, or even super man, when they will wage war on weaker germs of many forms.

Cosmic dust, through which the earth travels, spreads unknown diseases and death; it creates or destroys as conditions present themselves to this universal and everlasting power of germ life. It is the battle of parasites: the fittest will survive. We live because they need food and comfort. Before we can destroy them, they will have destroyed us — and they will live in a new storehouse furnished by us at a moment when they ruled us most. As a wasp innoculates a caterpiller with a state of suspended animation in order that its eggs may hatch successfully and its young feed leisurely upon the so-preserved feed bag, so are the parasites of life germs in us directing our fate unmistakably toward the fulfillment of their desires, their inevitable survival. One may ask, Why? But his cry will probably go unheeded, or be answered by the absolute truth, "You shall never know." What can we do about it? What can we do to rid ourselves of such pests? Nothing! We were never designed to be anything but a meal for parasites of all degrees. It could not be any different — a parasite's Garden of Eden, created and cultivated by parasites of a better grade. With all our medical and surgical science we are only creating "caterpillers" of a choice kind. Making human life immune to germs of a certain specie has never prevented a new "fog of death" from falling upon our race from the sky. It cannot be prevented, for no one can stop the earth's rotation or its speeding at a rate of eleven miles a second toward new constellations in the universe. No one can prevent the falling of cosmic dust impregnated with germs of ever-new varieties, new arrivals from space, with their baggage of instant or lingering death. Showers of meteorites are bombarding the earth constantly, silently bearing witness of the ever-changing cosmos: new lives for old; new creatures, weird, uncanny, and alien in their behavior; new germs for old; feasting upon what is, formulating what is to be.

## BEHOLD THE VALLEY OF THY SOUL

*Behold the valley of thy soul —*
*Drink from the mirror pool of thought,*
*Fathomless wisdom of the ages —*
*And so unveil the misty dawn of unknown,*
*Mysterious appearings of the Future*
*Retreat, remember if you can.*
*The puzzle of eternal life lies hidden there;*
*Creative measure well concealed*
*From consciousness of mortal man.*
*Thy soul alone can know the truth*
*And guide along a weary empty shell,*
*Until release has come in final meditation's bliss*
*To disappear once more*
*In thought's eternity.*

It is quite amusing to know that most of us humans profess some type of religion but that we forget its genesis and deep meaning, and more or less crucify the spirit of truth with material thoughts and worries. To be exact, we all worship the material, to some extent, instead of the living, invisible, and creative Thought Spirit. Only once in a great while it occurs to some of us, that in order to gain our material ends we must do some creative thinking, which is quite a hard task for some creatures. It is a long and winding road to learn the meaning of spiritual forces — some of us comprehend them with great difficulty; most of us, never quite understand the hidden language of Thought messages.

Through meditation it is possible for mortals to reach a certain psychic and clairvoyant view of the unknown and mysterious workings of the life-giving, creative Thought Spirit, for their own benefit and that of others. As long as they think in material terms exclusively, it is quite logical that no thought of a higher mental origin can penetrate into the arcane functions of the brain. Happiness depends entirely on one's thoughts. If a person thinks consistently of a material "Heaven," he will soon discover, that instead of being satisfied and happy, he lives in a purgatory of his own choice and making. He will suffer mental agony in trying hard to rid himself of the invisible shackles with which the material and finite Thought has enslaved him. The living, infinite Thought, which created man in the first place, can never be happy with the dead, material wishes and longings of a mortal body, in which it chooses to remain.

The true and living Thought must first of all cleanse man's mind of all that is unworthy, finite, material, and mortal, before it can lift itself and the creature once more into the realm of its own divine origin. Then all the wisdom is at once revealed to the living Thought, for it was created by this mysterious and baffling wisdom out of the reservoir of fathomless understanding into which it must return at the end of its mission. The Soul or Spirit of man is well informed of this mission which Thought is bringing him, when proper meditation has been accomplished. The temporary, selfish, material Thought in creatures like us makes it almost impossible for spiritual blessings and peace to do their fertile work. The true Thought, however, which is the creator of all things in the invisible realm, never rests; and it instantly destroys all selfish wishes for material surroundings if, through meditation, it is allowed to lead the mind to a higher mental level. Visions of what is yet to come, and of what we shall be like, are reward enough for those who earnestly seek to penetrate the veil of universal workings and creative life forces.

Thought which teaches us hidden meanings freely is eternal, and through blissful concentration it will uplift man's mind beyond the material into the realm of a spiritual, living existence, while yet in a mortal state, helping us to bear the burden of our earthbound bodies for the short spell of their existence. Already, humans can live here in the spiritual realm, and creative Thought supplies all their desires in super-abundance. So open your mind and let these invisible Thought forces penetrate into the mysteries of your brain, as you would open your eyes in order to read a book, and truth or God will reveal himself. That unknown force which man worships in his own queer way, calling it God and exhibiting his beliefs in so many confusing ceremonies in order to give it respect and fear, is always around us, like all things of normal origin. This God-force speaks to us in so many ways and approaches us with so many unfailing warnings as well as blessings, that it is really surprising to note how few people can truthfully say: "Yes, I am able to communicate with God, even to see and hear Him, without the common, artificial religious background." It seems as though many would rather worship a man-made gesture than a God who is in their very presence and is revealed by the forces of nature. In thunder and lightning, nature speaks in its loudest voice and puts on a magnificent spectacle, proving to man his own insignificance. Tornado, earthquake, and flood speak in another tone, dramatically, with the voice of God. In the various electrical and yet unknown rays which inhabit this cosmos, God makes no difference of distribution among selfish and foolish men. In the psychic region of telepathy and telepsychism from mind to mind, Thought flows freely, hoping for an understanding of the unknown. The voice of nature speaks in various color nuances and in musical compositions, which in turn are but a rebirth of materializating Thought into new shapes or sounds. There you cannot fail to see your God.

Your own body will soon become your temple and your daily religion. Within yourself you will discover sooner or later the bad (evil) or good (God). Learn to master psychic reactions, which play on your mind and Soul as a master musician plays on his instrument; and truth and enlightenment will lead you toward the elusive secrets of life. Meditation, your teacher, shows you the way to the stars, to silence and happiness, without asking for dues or rewards. All the good things in life are free, to those who know where to look for them and how to benefit by them. Being merely tiny units of the universal riddle, we must adopt and humbly accept the natural, godly life intended for us, and must reject the artificial and over-civilized state of modern barbarism which leads to evil, destruction, and death. The natural life is a life of truth and of good deeds, a life which bears fruit when it has exchanged ignorance — the greatest sin of mankind — for knowledge and everlasting happiness.

# CLAIRVOYANT — PROPHESY

*The beauty of the mysterious*
*Is the true source of inspirations,*
*Coming to man in prophetic dreams and*
*Thought transmissions from the unknown,*
*Invisible intelligence out of another*
*Dimension, helping tiny man to build*
*His kind of civilization, with its art*
*And science for the benefit of*
*Generations to come.*

SPIRIT and Thought crystallize in men when time and place are right. To adopt a shape commonly found on this earth or on other planets is perhaps the only way in which Thought may manifest itself. The carpenter's Son understood this when he said, "In my father's house are many mansions." The house is the universe, the mansions are the numerous planets. In other words, if we are here now in the shape of human beings, it is because the invisible Thought Spirit chose us— he wanted to live in us as long as our mortal body permits. To revere man for his deeds is entirely wrong and ignorant. Thought, passing through the body like an electric current and leaving its lasting effect on the brain capacity, is alone responsible for man's accomplishments. Without the spiritual, invisible Thought guidance we might still be sub-barbaric creatures. But beause of the fertilizing effect of the mysterious Thought ray which penetrated the skull and the brain of the early evolutionary creatures, we have developed enormously, and this present stage of our existence is quite different from the genetic stage. It has yet to be shown to what level of advancement the creature called man, possessing this godly power of Thought concentration, may ascend.

The eternal Thought, after leaving a body which has outworn its usefulness, can adopt any shape of creation, or can enter another human body. This will explain the mystery of the occasional child prodigy who possesses unusual knowledge without having had the time and experience usually necessary for gaining that knowledge. A genius is probably a person in whom the Thought vibrations are active in a super-abundant way, whose brain cells collect wisdom in much the same manner as bees gather honey. There are great reservoirs of intelligence filled with Thought forces which have left various beings over thousands of years, beings who lived not only in our world but also on other planets. This intelligence may be gathered into certain chosen individuals by means of Thought transmission, thus making them prodigies or geniuses.

Thought cannot be measured by time or space, and it matters but little where it had its beginning. The important fact is that it is there — all powerful, invisible, eternal—and that anyone may easily contact it. Religionists call this their God and they finally succeeded in making a person out of it, a being which we humans are supposed to fear. And they put it beyond the reach of mortal imagination by clothing it in all sorts of weird ceremonies. Jesus said, "God is Spirit"; he did not make a person out of it. The brain charges Thought no admission, no fine for trespassing. The good Thought — or God — is free, as are all the best things in life. We do not need fear, hellfire, or other such thoughts created for the benefit of superstition. All Thought is eternal and cannot be burned by imaginary, man-made hellfire, invented by an unscrupulous few in order to induce fear and obedience. We are all children of mother nature, which is good and all good things were created in an invisible Thought realm, which is a godly realm, to be sure, and worthy of worship.

This natural godly law created universes with their millions of suns, planets, moons, and asteroids, floating in an orderly, organized system, through infinite space — and it created the microscopic beauty of germ life, of which we humans are a part. In its infinite wisdom, it takes care of all, occasionally letting us know, by Thought communion, just how futile it is to worry our poor heads over an existence quite insignificant in comparison to the myriad of creations which inhabit the starry sky. For the inspired few, "Heaven" is understood, and direct communication has been established with God power through the medium of thought. Meditating men shall see the light, using Thought power for the cornerstone upon which to build new civilizations. If man fails to see truth at such beneficial and divine moments, then he is a mere automaton, a creature without thinking faculties and will power. There are many of these, sadly so, but it is not entirely their fault. Others robbed them of the only thing worth while— the Soul or Spirit— and left them derelict sombies, until nature releases what is left of them.

The thousands of differing opinions of men as to what God looks like and what He may do to us, have left many people quite hopeless in the beliefs which selfish, scheming fanatics feed their minds for the price of money. These poor souls have forgotten that they can do their own philosophic thinking without interference by anyone, most certainly without danger of hellfire. But some of them simply refuse to believe in scientific truths and common sense; they would rather live in constant fear of home-made purgatory. Their own thoughts created that invisible hell, and it finally materialized into their existence, torturing their imaginations and leading them literally into a state of hell. They invited evil thought domination, and it is getting the best of them. They could be free, if they wanted it so, by letting the true and good Thought into their brain cells and thus finding immediate relief. One cannot obey two masters at one and the same time. One can obey only *one* thought faithfully, the Thought of good or the thought of evil. Jesus said, "What I do, ye shall do also." He chased the evil spirits or thoughts away from the possessed victims. You shall do the same — the bad thoughts need not get the best of you, unless you want it thus. There is enough godly Thought power in you to chase away all evil thought units.

The reason why so many people cannot understand the truth is that their brain cells do not operate properly for the reception of simple, eternal truths. No one could possibly expect a caveman to know how to operate a radio, a car, or an airplane. A water glass can be filled only to its own capacity. It is quite the same with the human brain. Evolution has developed us to the point where we can understand the principle behind a radio, a car, or an airplane. So nobody with common sense can possibly blame a caveman for smashing the radio because of his superstitious fear, for wrecking the car and burning the airplane because he is not able to understand the working principle of such modern machinery.

The same applies to the psychic and clairvoyant thoughts of certain humans. They are leaps into the future and must be treated as such. Controlled and directed by Thought units of an unknown frequency, such persons see in visions and dreams, with a clarity known only to themselves, things which are yet to come. They are prophetic in their utterances; they speak not in the language of the average individual, but are at certain times highly charged with the mysterious power of Thought waves. In reality, there is nothing supernatural about this. It just happens, that a certain advanced Thought crystallized and took form in the brain cells, revealing to us the power behind a Thought.

Jesus knew what he meant when he said, "Forgive them, for they know not what they do." Only a few understood His message of good will. All prophetic Thoughts passing through the brain of man, leaving behind unknown wisdom, have first been ridiculed, then persecuted, and the carrier of such Thought has often been ruthlessly killed. Even today such is being done. Time has not changed human nature. People still crucify in their own way anyone whom they cannot comprehend and whom they fear because of their ignorance. As Buddha quotes: "Ignorance is the greatest sin," and so it is easy to understand just why persecutions will always exist. It is the ignorant persons, the ones with the brain capacity of cavemen, who destroy everything they cannot comprehend, quite forgetting that by killing the body they cannot eliminate Thought also. Thought will come back in others until the message has been fully understood. That is where wisdom lies. Truth must rule even if it takes an eternity to convince mortals of the absurdity of killing anyone who carries dynamic truth principles which are indestructable, eternal, and of godly origin. These principles were created long before the germ of human kind found its way to this planet.

Humans who impulsively criticize, persecute, and kill, whether for political, religious, or other reasons, deserve pity. They do not know that the eternal wisdom cannot be exterminated by hatred and fanatical actions against mortal man. Thought will live when all matter seems dead. Thought vibrations, created in an invisible realm, in another dimension, can be elminated only when contacted in that same dimension, through the medium of concentration and sincere meditation. Spiritual law cannot be measured in human terms; it is beyond the reach of human punishment, and it always triumphs over anything in the flesh. It *was* there —before the first man looked with awe and admiration toward the stars. It *is* here — always with us, around us — helping us carry on, provided we want it so, free for anyone on this planet. It *will* be there long after the last man has left earth and found other planets for his habitation in order that he may carry on the perpetuation of his own species, directed and guided by the cosmic forces of Thought radiation. It *will* be there if all cosmos were to be wiped away into nothing and then molded all over again into weird, incomprehensible shapes as if to demonstrate the flexibility and power of eternal thus divine Thought. That it *is* we should feel and see in the life of our every day experience. Just where and when it originated is not necessary for us to know as long as we live by and with it for the short span allotted to earthlings.

## GOD IS . . .

God is life-giving and sustaining cosmic radiation projected through space, reaching in a most beneficial manner everyone who believes in its creative power. Where there is light, darkness cannot prevail. Yes cannot be no. Good cannot be evil. The force that created darkness, disease, and death is an evil one, created by disobedience of natural laws. Everything and everyone acting according to the exalted natural law is within reach of the benefits of its cosmic radiation. All who oppose it invite punishment in the form of disease and final death. We are the undisputed product of nature and cannot possibly act contrary to such divine law and still expect to remain healthy in mind and body. People could go on living indefinitely if they would but recognize and use the power of natural law. It is easier to believe in a lie than to worship truth. That is perhaps the reason why there is so much unhappiness and sickness on this earth. The truth is too simple, and that's why it is hard to find and even harder to believe. In reality, no one can be persecuted for believing truth, but always force is used to induce people to believe lies. The truth is contrary to a lie, and one cannot have room in the other.

Cosmic radiation is force projected for good to all within reach of its influence. Nothing can survive in absolute darkness and cold. The forces which project darkness and death are of evil and destructive origin. Persons of sound mind had better not tamper with wicked radiation, no matter from what source it has been released. Religionists have their names for both these forces, calling them God and Devil, expecting us to believe in fairy tales, illusions and hallucinations. If, perchance, mankind had never heard of such confusing and contradicting theories, it would have evolved on a more or less scientific point of view, analyzing truth as it is and worry not about any supernatural revealed religion.

It does not matter much just how, where, and when forces of evil and good were and are projected upon us. We now know that they are responsible for our being here as well as for our remaining here. That fact is important. There are rays and waves floating through space — many not even yet suspected — doing evil and good to creatures like us. To ignore their presence is ignorant, and will certainly not nullify their existence. Science tells us that the cosmic ray may in some way be responsible for everything created throughout the universe, which includes planet earth. Of course, knowledge of this would offset the theory of supernatural, revealed religion which has been fed to man for many a century; so people ignore such truthful information. But the cosmic ray exists, nevertheless, caring very little what opinion man may have of its existence and its power.

It would have been quite a blessing to "homo erectus" of never having heard the siren call of the "Mother Church" with its corrupting and racketeering influence upon the mind. Not having heard, man would positively act more in accordance with natural laws and thus be nearer to truth and God. As a little child knows nothing of any church God until influenced by such a thought, it grows according to natural law, which is of God and in which all of us have our being. No church organization, no matter how powerful, can tamper with or duplicate the supreme laws of nature. In the name of Christ, the clergy has only one object in mind — that is, to dominate the human race by robbing it of its mentality and preventing it from finding truth. In the name of God they are raising the Devil all over this earth and will continue to do so until enough true spiritual power or common sense has been released upon mankind to destroy the Antichrist. Most deliberately the soul of man is being led away from life-giving and sustaining God power, is being given darkness, despair, superstition, and hellfire instead, and is told not to dispute theological views. There is absolutely nothing church religion has to offer while people are yet alive. Everything seems to be prepared for them, however, and will materialize, so they claim, in the hereafter, in an especially chosen place esteemed for a comparative few. Well, we all know that we are very much alive right now and here, and whatever weird power may be responsible for our existence will also partake in our well-being and prosperity. "As you desire, so shall it be unto you," a great spiritual teacher said long ago. This man well knew what he was saying. In other words: "If you but concentrate on the eternal power coming to us from space, and have an absolute faith in its invisible workings, all things within reason will materialize as desired." That is the stuff prayers are made of — a simple yet forceful desire, without any religious hocus-pocus. "As I do so shall ye do also, and better." Understanding this divine message, I fail to see just how any creature still insists on paying for any kind of religious thinking. "According to your faith be it unto you." One who has lost his faith in mother nature certainly will not find it in any church organization. By contacting spiritual law through meditation, oneness with God will be reestablished, and once more faith in nature and its mysterious workings will predominate.

The first four-legged creature, using his hind legs for walking purposes exclusively, permitting the front legs to become useful tools, must have created quite a sensation. He was an inspiring example to others of his kind, and so fascinated them that they adopted the new fashion. Whatever prompted this creature to experiment thus with his own body came close to a divine inspiration. It was a pioneering Thought of astounding and far reaching results, an example of the superiority of invisible Thought over visible matter. Civilization as such would be quite unthinkable if we still used four legs to transport our bodies instead of two. Whatever force was responsible for this progress is still responsible for all things created here on earth, and also for such things that have yet to materialize. A remarkable force it must be, creating life in so many forms, sustaining them all in its own queer way. Death certainly cannot have any part in such a stupendous scheme of things. Death as such has never existed and is but a transformer of matter. A caterpillar does not die; he goes through a state of transmutation, before he becomes a glorious winged insect. We are not caterpillars in the sense of the word; however, all of us know well that our bodies are but mortal and in order to be transformed must rest quite still for a while. "It doth not yet appear what we shall be." None shall see God's face and yet live. This something, this power, is too immense for any comprehension, especially with a brain of our making. We cannot grasp completely the laws of nature. That is the reason why none can possibly see that law with mortal eyes. Jesus said, "God is Spirit." This spiritual God law has no face of any kind. It is a universal law, has been and will be, even after man will long be forgotten on this planet. Those who doubt the great cosmic power which holds the atoms as well as the farthest nebulae in firm control will die a quick mental death. Their thoughts will not be picked up by any with sufficient brain capacity. It is a pity that so many people still follow the old and worm eaten way of superstition. Their way of thinking is largely responsible for the periodic stampede of human cattle into war, depression, mass hallucinations, religious persecution. Systematically mankind is being robbed of the holy faculty left in its defense — the ability to judge for themselves between true and false.

Evil of such calibre will be permitted as long as it can be absorbed by creatures with evil inclinations. It will disappear, and never be mentioned again, as soon as the human mind is capable and willing to be directed by the more beneficial cosmic and divine Thought radiation pentrating into their brain cells, reacting for good exclusively. Then, and only then, the reign of good — God — truth — or what have you — will overpower all opposition, no matter under what disguise it has been represented to man. Until then, these pioneers of truth and science will suffer untold misery and violence, physically as well as mentally, for daring to teach truth as it is, due to the slow mental evolution through which the human race must pass. Outcasts, lonely, misunderstood, misrepresented, and persecuted, are these mental pioneers who are carriers of the mysterious life beam by which advanced knowledge may be gained. Their constant contact with the psychic force enables them to tell of things to come, to visualize and outline them as though they had materialized already. "My kingdom is not of this world," may be fully understood by those who gaze into the future with their uncanny, inner vision, whose psychic power through meditation has penetrated the workings of spiritual, cosmic law — coming to them like a "flash from Heaven" as the religionists would want you to believe. The vast difference, however, between the religionist and the scientific thinker is that the religionist's "Heaven" is somewhere prepared in his imagination, whereas the scientific thinker knows very well that the earth floats at unerring and tremendous speed onwards in space, or "Heaven," if you please. I fail to see where it is necessary to enter into two heavens, when we are already traveling through heaven all the time. Cosmic power is released in all directions, consuming with its life-giving and creative principles anything in its path, the earth being no exception. Humans lack faith in a perfect and natural law. They hate to exchange it for their old-fashioned faith in an adopted church God who is constantly burning them with Hell Fire while still alive. They would rather worship by fear and superstition the invisible ruler of doubt and evil. Even a tree has more common sense than many of the "highest form of life" can ever possess. A tree waits patiently for the sun rays to create new life, in the form of protoplasm, which is so essential for its survival. It seems to understand, in its own way, that after rain, snow, cold, storm, and night, sunlight will conquer all. Neither does a tree jump out of the ground in order to follow the sun in its path, possessed by a greedy desire to swallow all the light for himself. Somehow the tree knows that such a method would be suicidal. Trees, therefore, are not so stupid or greedy as man.

Since the cockroach has survived for the last twenty million years and still remains in its original shape, why is it that man worries over a miserly fifty or sixty years of life? It is because the lowly insect acts according to natural laws which provide all necessities while living, whereas man forever worries his head over problems not meant for him in the first place.

Faith is essential to life. Without it there is oblivion. Life remains life— even if it is the life of a bug. To an insect, life is just as important as your own to you. All life has been created by the same living force and will be sustained in its own manner, right here and now. Nature grants no special favors; neither are there any reservations made here or in the "beyond." Nature is no respecter of creeds, notions, and commotions. It could not be so and still remain immutable law, disregarding love and hate and certainly not giving "Heaven" to those who peddle lies. The inspired, psychic Son of a carpenter understood spiritual and cosmic law one hundred per cent when he said, "I am with you alway, even unto the end of the world." Only by understanding the miracle of spiritual Thought messages can we be free to choose good from evil and to build civilization there upon.

## ATLANTIS

WHAT is it that compels the little two-legged termite, man, to forge ahead — often in the face of defeat — to conquer, dominate, and rule on this planet, striving in all earnest toward a higher level of civilzation? Is it because he wishes to know what is beyond, that man walks determinedly the long, weary, blood-soaked path of evolution? Perhaps man resents the fact that he is but a certain type of animal, and therefore combines all his thinking capacity and will power in an effort to shake off the hide of his ape ancestors. Man has improved his habitation on earth. He no longer hides in caves, cold, fearful, and always hungry for the blood and flesh of his enemies. Ancient civilization has disappeared since, leaving behind silent witnesses of men's achievements and genius — concerning an art and a style of architecture unsurpassed even by modern science. This modern age is still learning eagerly from the achievements of past races which were far superior to our present ones. Stone monuments and priceless carvings are a silent, powerful tribute to man's conquests of the past, and challenge men today to surpass all that once existed.

The science of Atlantis affords an awe-inspiring motive even today to jealous man. It has never been exactly duplicated, and scientists all over the globe are baffled by the amazing brain function of the educated Atlantian. It is said of these people that they were in constant communication with intelligent creatures from outer space such as Mars, Venus, and Mercury. How else was it possible for them to know the secret of overcoming gravity, of splitting and using atomic power, when we of today are still amateurs in these arts? Who instructed the scientists of Atlantis, and what remarkable process of brain functioning was responsible for allowing these ancient wizards to comprehend all that was taught them? Did all, or most, of the Atlantians perish beneath a blanket of water, thus writing a finish to this ingenious race? By astronomical calculation they knew that their homeland would in time undergo a change, due to the flexibility of the earth axis. It was known to them that this change would mean submersion of the continent in the Atlantic Ocean. The average person of that time regarded the coming catastrophe as a flood of water, and the story has come down to this day and is recorded in the Bible. Without this knowledge of coming events, the Atlantians would have been unable to carry their kind of civilization into the far-off regions of Egypt and Central America, thus establishing the Mayan Empire. In their worship, art, and architecture, both Egypt and the Mayan Empire betray Atlantian origin.

It is impossible to believe that with all their wisdom they were unable to escape the calamity which befell their continent. Does it not seem more plausible to assume that a small remnant of master scientists had in readiness for an emergency of the kind anticipated space cruisers which would carry them safely to the nearest planet? After adapting themselves to conditions on such a planet, they may have combined their knowledge with that of the intelligent creatures living there.

Who will deny that perhaps we of today are subconsciously instructed by a psychic Thought radiation, or an educational super radio beam directed by such creatures in space? Intelligent people today are familiar with the theory of a reservoir of Thought somewhere in space. Scientists admit that there is thinking matter in the ether. It is also admitted that creatures on neighboring planets are trying constantly to make themselves understood by means of code messages which we are as yet unable to decipher. Whatever we cannot understand is called static noises on the radio. It is, however, very likely that within the nucleus of the so-called static lies the key to interplanetary communication. Again the Atlantians showed superior thinking ability, in analyzing such messages and in using them to their own advantage. Today we are but sad imitators of a lost science.

This is perhaps another good reason why we keep on trying to achieve greater things and to gain entrance into the heritage of wisdom. The urge to amount to something, to go on a mission, exists in every earthling of sound mind. Aided by the constant Thought radiations coming to us from somewhere in space, we may some day surpass the old Atlantians in wisdom. In a quiet, meditative, expectant mood, man envisions his destiny, and he will never rest until he has seen with mortal eyes the fulfillment of his visions, dreams, or inspired Thought revelations. Man, the super animal, neurotic, restless, tries hard to better his lot on this planet. With the aid of psychic ability, he is instructed of things and events which otherwise would escape his notice. Men are able to tune in on the reservoir of Thoughts from far off space, to receive messages let us assume from Atlantians who were given up for lost but who somehow did survive and who now are guiding man's destiny, molding his character, giving assurance that Thought can never die. Perhaps Atlantians often referred to as being the "Sons of the Gods" urge man in the name of science, to conquer all or nothing; make him understand how little he is and yet how big he can be if he practices love instead of merely preaching about it. Truth can prevail only by banishing inherited fear of the mysterious and by giving psychic knowledge to all mankind. As time rolls by, perhaps the human race may be forced, as were the Atlantians, to migrate to another planet. History may repeat itself in the not so distant future, and as the Atlantians had to think fast in their days of distress so may we. Life is a state of constant war, a relentless, unmerciful, bitter struggle, a survival of the fittest. Preparedness for all eventualities is the Thought which Atlantis left with us as a silent, dynamic lesson.

At the present time, however, science is busily engaged — wasting precious time and materials — in devising chemicals and weapons for the destruction of man rather than for the advancement of the species. But here and there a change of Thought is hitting home. All energy, skill, and common sense must combine to put an end to the self-mutilation of the human brotherhood. The scientific age, a new order, is here to stay. It is unerringly pressing toward a goal, defying superstition, and building for man his dreams of a paradise on earth. Soon science will be building space cars, visit neighboring worlds, learning what can and will be useful to us, tearing the heavens asunder, looking after the many mansions in the Father's house. It is not weeping like Alexander the Great, for there *are* more worlds to conquer in the name of a sane, scientific state of existence. Perhaps some day the riddle of Atlantis and its sacrifice for a just cause will be understood; and millions of earthlings may find happiness in the new order of scientific enlightenment. And all this was made possible, perhaps, by the Atlantians who survived, who perpetuated themselves and their wisdom, and who now instruct us via Thought messages.

"The eternal light," symbolizing Atlantian worship, signifies wisdom, tolerance, and life itself; is still burning, invisible to man's eye, yet ever enlightening his Spirit in the subconscious and guiding him by Thoughts, visions, and prophetic dreams, as it did in days past in old Atlantis where truth was paramount and where "The eternal light" meant things good, godly, and worth suffering for. Where there is light, darkness must vanish, including all belief in superstition, with its customary fanatical tendencies. Mankind went through many ages similar to the one known as the Dark Age, with its mediaeval voodoos and ignorances, when free Thought was surpressed by means of torture and inquisition. Yet the principle of "The eternal light" was carried on by humans who had a burning desire for scientific facts and who courageously laid down their lives for it, knowing that their sacrifice would not be in vain, knowing that others would carry on the work and Thought by which they had been inspired. Today we are beginning to drift more freely than ever before toward the glories existing in our highest expectations and dreams. Where there is light, the opposing forces of evil must melt like snow in the sun. They can no longer be harmful, nor keep man from his never-ending progress in building a new order. Thus man shall enjoy the fruit of his labor and leave the laggard and the straggler behind. Let these enjoy the foolish notions of growing the trees of life by their leaves instead from their roots, if they will. They shall thus be left to their childlike illusions concerning their various types of theology and politics; they may keep on slaughtering one another over hair-splitting differences of opinion. But science will carry on even if it has to abandon this planet in its search for peace and happiness and leave this world to the sons of men, or super animals, isolating itself by a vast wall of space in order never to be molested again.

## MENTAL DYNAMITE: WORDS

"IN the beginning was the Word [Logos] and the Word was with God, and the Word was God," John 1:1. Jesus said distinctly "God is Spirit: and they that worship him must worship him in spirit and in truth." Jesus in John 6:63, said, "It is the spirit that quickeneth: the flesh profiteth nothing: the words that I speak unto you, they are spirit, and they are life." The dictionary quotes *Logos* as "The Thought."

Since Logos and the Word are the same, then God must have employed Thought, Logos, or the power of the Word to create all things. If Thought, Logos, or the Word are of spiritual and invisible origin, and have been there from the beginning, then Thought, Word, or Logos, are God all in one. Ja-veh, or Jehovah, said to the Israelities: "I am the Lord thy God... thou shalt have no other gods before me." No one can see Thought. God said, "There shall no man see me and live." Thought (Logos) has no face of any kind, and need not have in order to convince mortals of its power. The only way we can communicate with God is through the channels of Thought. If humans would but realize this point, man-made religion would loose its strangle hold from them because the truth makes us free. All Biblical characters, prophets, etc., communicated with and understood God by means of Thought exclusively, in the same way that all of us receive Thought messages from the eternal reservoir of Thought or God. The only difference is that most of us hate to listen to the "still small voice." It cannot be denied that man has received inspired messages, leading to inventions and discoveries, which came to him like a flash from Heaven all through the ages. All this adds to the mysterious greatness of the invisible, life-giving, cosmic Thought radiation.

The so-called pagans worshipped the sun, the moon, and the stars as the giver of life. Hammurabi, King of Babylon, 2250 B.C., practised sun worship. The ancient people of Atlantis had faith in "The Eternal Light." The Egyptian sun god was Ra, and the Bible records in Ezekiel 8:16 that five and twenty men worshipped the sun towards the east, at the door of the temple of the Lord. The Aryan race, coming from the Caucasus, saw in the sun their creator, preserver, and savior. The Mayan race of Central America, and the Incas of Peru, were sun worshippers. Japan, even today, has for its national emblem the symbol of the rising sun. According to Webster's dictionary, the name Sunday has its origin in an adoration of the sun by the ancient races of earth.

According to Genesis 1:3, 4, and 5, God created light on the first day. The only force sufficiently powerful to give light and warmth to the earth is the sun. Her energy causes the earth to rotate, thus giving it day and night. It takes eight minutes for sunlight to span the gulf of space between earth and sun. Thus in the beginning the earth must have been without the benefit of any sunlight for a period of eight minutes. We can imagine the state of this planet at that time, since it is scientifically known that the absence of sunlight for even one minute is sufficient to freeze any living thing into solid ice. In Genesis 1:16, 17, and 18, the Bible goes on to say that God made the sun and moon on the fourth day. The good soul who recorded this bit of information certainly got mixed up somewhere, because this is next to impossible. Without the sun to cause a first day and a first night, there could never have been a second, third, fourth, or any day at all. If Jehovah is light — then He must have created the sun first, unless the sun is also Jehovah, causing the trinity of light, love, and life in contrast to the trinity of darkness which is evil, disease, and death. This reveals a perfectly natural law — light and life on one side, and darkness and destruction on the other. Perhaps that is the reason for sun worship. Zoroaster did not worship the sun itself, but rather its spiritual, life-giving effect on living things. Science regards humans as absorbers of solar energy, not unlike plants which produce protoplasm with the aid of sunlight.

Jesus did not center his faith on the object of the sun, as other saviors before him. He tried to make people universe conscious by saying, "In my father's house [universe] are many mansions [planets]." This theory Newton later confirmed with his calculations. With the aid of the two hundred inch telescope, an entirely new conception will arrive; and when we begin to comprehend the vastness of the universes, with their suns and planets, we will have a glimpse of what God really looks like. Every scientific discovery concerning the cosmos adds to the greatness of the mysterious life radiation throughout space, a radiation divine and godly, to be sure. The law governing this stupendous force is not respecter of persons, thus it is available to all. In this power we have our being, regardless of our belief or disbelief. This earth of ours speeds on in its endless journey at eleven miles per second, unnoticed by us. Truly remarkable must be such a law, to prevent chaos and collision among the innumerable suns, planets, and comets which stay in order in the heavens with unerring precision. But man has little faith in what he cannot possibly understand, and he centers all his activities in his own ego. He is, in general, quite unaware that should the master clock of the universe fail but once for a fraction of a second, his existence would be one of eternal doom. He goes on wondering whether it is possible for him to enter heaven in the hereafter which is promised to him for faithful fulfillment of all the requirements made of him by religionists; and he forgets the fact that he is floating and always will float in heaven or space. It is truly said, "All good things in life are free." So is eternal life free for anyone who will accept it. Where else can one go from here but to heaven? There is no other place prepared for planets, with humans clinging parasitically to them, to rotate in. It is the truth which shall make you free, and not fear ridden, man-made, religious hellfire.

## MEDITATION

When one's Soul enters the final process of transformation, caused by physical absence of life, it will be ready to take to space or heaven on spiritual wings, fearlessly leaving a valley of death and desolation, searching out one's Soul vibration, by matching the rhythm of the eternal Voice coming with unerring skill and speed from the pool of Thought, where rest and peace welcomes a Soul — lonely, tired from humiliating effects of mental browbeating and spiritual crucifixion — to forget and erase the slight error of choosing the body of an animal — man — for a temporary domicile on a planet called earth.

We are all part of a universal principle — Light, Love, Life — which spells: God — Spirit — Truth.

Wanderers in darkness, persecuted for spiritual enlightenment and mental pioneering, we build a living unit in an eternal cycle of cosmic transformation.

> *Behold the valley of thy soul —*
> *Drink from the mirror pool of thought,*
> *Fathomless wisdom of the ages —*
> *And so unveil the misty dawn of unknown,*
> *Mysterious appearings of the Future*
> *Retreat, remember if you can.*
> *The puzzle of eternal life lies hidden there;*
> *Creative measure well concealed*
> *From consciousness of mortal man.*

*Thy soul alone can know the truth*
*And guide along a weary empty shell,*
*Until release has come in final meditation's bliss*
*To disappear once more*
*In thought's eternity.*

## CONCENTRATION

CONCENTRATION, or the compass of success, makes you master of fate. Knowing the power of the spoken word as a manifestation of Thought, I will now quote several important words which, when used in conjunction with the "I am," bring into play the unseen, psychic forces, for your personal benefit.

*Health, Wealth, Wisdom, Power, Force, Youth, Energy, Peace, Poise, Harmony, Good Will, Intelligence, Justice, Law, Order, Discipline, Inspiration, Happiness, Success, Purpose, Persistence, Spirit, Truth, Faith, Science, Confidence, Mastery, Radiation, Fearless, Reincarnation, Clairvoyance.*

The objective mind will often wander in wrong directions, and it must be controlled and guided toward an aim. Then wandering will gradually lessen and finally stop, making you master of concentration. As such you then live within the law of the universal voice, in the stillness of the psychic realm of Thought. Let the outer mind become servant, not master, for each word in conjunction with the "I" becomes a wasted power unit if related unwisely to others. Thought is ammunition; use it for, not against your purpose. Silence and survey are golden portals through which achievement must pass on its way toward recognition and materialization of one's ambitions and ideals. Through the medium of concentration the soul is free to search for nourishing Thoughts; it is well to set aside time for mental exercise after each day's activities, to regain lost force.

"I am the beginning and the end," says the Lord. Without the "I" there would not be life-consciousness in any shape or form; there would be only desolation and death. You are the "I" — a unit within a thinking cosmos, accounting for its law and order. Be aware of the vital life force coming to you after blissful meditation on harmonious Thought power, released anew for the benefit of the "I", thus sanctifying the radiant, inner voice. Alone under a star-lit sky, in a forest, or on the ocean during tempest, one feels at home with all that is. A spiritual union is almost completed, after the realization of one's material insignificance. It seems as though the Thought units cry out for release from man's brain cells, so that they may rush back to the reservoir of eternal bliss in that spiritual realm of existence which we mortals only occasionally have the fortitude to look upon. In these rare moments, priceless bliss is attained — free — godly — which guides the mental pioneer in an effort to clear away the mist of superstition and fear of the unknown, and to bring about true spiritual happiness which is essential for the survival of a people earthbound by material environment and habits. "As in Heaven, so on earth" is the desire of those who live in the inspired atmosphere and who hold their peace with a restless world, for the sake of contentment and happiness.

Most inventions are the product of an ability to think constructively. Mental evolution will set the man of the future far above the average person of today who will certainly seem "semi-barbaric" in contrast with the spiritual outlook, refinements, science, industrial relations, and even physical appearance of the man who is yet to be. To be godlike, and not warlike, is the aim of the prophetic, mental pioneer of today, who envisions an age of supreme spiritual rulership organized for the best of all concerned. The Thoughts of today will be the reality of tomorrow. If man will concentrate in an effort to become master of himself and his circumstances, he can draw enough power out of the mysterious realm of Thought to realize and to sustain a better existence right here on earth; he need not wait for a hereafter to supply his needs, for heaven on earth lies within the reach of all who honestly desire it.

## SOUND AND LIGHT

PHYSICALLY we are propagated star dust. Sound and light give eyes and ears to animated particles and form them into the various shapes necessary to preserve and sustain life on this planet. Through the medium of sound and light we are able to grasp subconsciously the hidden meanings of spiritual origin and existence. The innumerable sound effects upon human ears stimulate the connection between the subconscious and the conscious existence of man. The cry of a babe starts the thought of inquiry into the child's welfare. The sound of drums arouses humans into a frenzy of war-like behavior. The church organ produces a most amazing effect upon listeners, bringing about docile and beneficial emotions. Symphony orchestras, jazz bands, all dance music, produce a weird effect, release thoughts, and create actions accordingly. There are sounds that will strike terror into superstitious minds — the noise of thunder, the rumble of a volcano, cannons, guns, the screech of an owl, the howl of a wolf.

Light is responsible for the progress of a race, its religion, its civilization. Besides heat, it produces colors which stimulate the artist, poet, and philosopher to think and wonder about the effects of light upon the mind of man. The sight of sunset, the Aurora Borealis, or northern lights, the midnight sun, lightning — all start within us a God consciousness, a leaning toward the realm of unseen Thought. The sight of a starlit night, an erupting vocano, or fire, arouse different feelings. Some of them make us passive; others change our mood into violence.

Sound and light are unpaid teachers of law and truth, survival and eternity. They are God's servants, instructing all who are willing to be instructed. Thought, Love, God, cannot be destroyed by sword, fire, and poison; they are of another dimension and of eternal duration. The spiritual inner man is a part of God through his ability of Thought communion by which he gains faith, overcomes fear, and creates an undying spiritual unity with the Father. The voice universal constantly vibrates with the "inner self," "astral body," or the subconscious man, as another form of sound audible only to the psychic chosen. Without an inner illumination caused by the inner voice — which directs mortals away from material follies and desires toward everlasting bliss, a sort of Nirvana — it is quite impossible to know the living God within us.

All heavenly bodies cast into the ether vibrations or sounds which are picked up, as a form of static, on sound detectors or radios, and which influence the mind of man and render him helpless against the forecs of nature which are beyond his understanding. Once a tiny atom has found its way into a human being, what can it know about the gigantic shape in which it is traveling? Yet if the hidden power within that atom were to be released, it would probably blow its carrier to more atoms. In size, man might well be compared with a living, inspired atom floating about within a giant of space. The earth, in turn, may be but an atom in the solar systems within the cosmos.

The eternal order of things does not permit man to

expect complete annihilation but to expect survival in the form of stardust, eternity in God, the Father. He is that creative, spiritual power in whom we live and move and have our being, in whom disease and death are but a state of transmutation or non-existent, makes us a part of Himself and thus entitles us to spiritual survival. Sound and light tell of the glory of Spirit over matter, and sound out an age-old song of praise, a symphony of universal beauty and lasting charm, in which planets, suns, and moons are notes in the master composition. Played in a harmonious, spiritual manner upon the minds of all in creation, it illumines with dazzling color the non-existence of time, the infinity of space, and helps man to get in tune with the spiritual spark within him, so that he may stand erect, without fear, as a true nucleus of God's infinity and wisdom.

Know Him who is all, and worries will dissolve, fear will disappear, disease and death will be no more, conflict, strife and warfare will vanish, and eternal happiness will take their place. Those who live within the Spirit are in accordance with natural law, and they will succeed where others fail. Those who obey the spiritual inner voice are truly Sons of God and are always welcomed. Vibrations for good register within him who listens to the still small voice, in accordance with the law of compensation which rewards faith and truth. If, during our journey on earth, our thoughts are directed toward things desirable, these will materialize in due time. "As a man thinketh, so shall he be." If one always thinks of hellfire and death, he will surely burn and die. One cannot plant a cactus and expect to reap peaches. Plant the seed of hate in the spiritual realm of Thought, and you will soon see what happens. Natural law never changes. With faith in such a law, it is useless to dig day after day into the ground in an effort to discover why a seed has not yet produced a tree. The spiritual Thought seed obeys the same law. In due time, if watered with spiritual faith and respectful waiting, and not disturbed by worry, fear, and doubt, Thought will blossom and bear fruit when least expected. "As in heaven, so on earth" will come true if enough concentrated Thought seeds are planted in the divine realm of Thought by earthlings; then a state of heaven on earth will be visible to all mankind. Without spiritual peace, one cannot expect material peace. The thoughts of men are still bent on destruction, and the products of such thoughts are cannons, battleships, poison gas, bombing planes, germ warfare, and atom bombs. If more and more people will accept the subconscious flow of good Thought, they will soon act constructively and will bring the inspired kingdom into its own. Thought vibrations rule this universe. They come to us via space, and produce sounds audible to our inner detector, Soul, or Spirit. By means of a mysterious psychic power, they travel like a flash of invisible light and penetrate the subconsciousness of the inner man who alone is capable of absorbing the hidden meanings of a "Mene tekle" from a spiritual God substance.

## MAN — THE SUPER ANIMAL

MAN searches to rediscover the secret of life, after having lost it because of its simplicity. Although he is a living example of the formula "life," he believes he can create it synthetically. He is the carrier of life, the channel through which life is created, but he refuses to know himself. Such is man, the "overlord" of all that is in existence on the planet earth. Man plays his little game, strives to be great because he is small, and tries to fool others, but succeeds only in fooling himself with his "civilized" ideas which hide the beast he truly is. He professes sincerity but is in reality a hypocrite; he preaches love, but practices hate; he builds temples and modern "Babylonian Towers," only to show his skill in destroying them at unbalanced moments with his pet hobby, war. He wears clothes to hide the hideous ape he represents. He believes in a righteous God, but worships mammon, vice, corruption, and the rest of Satan's brood. He expects eternal life as a reward for his endless persecutions, terrorism, and warfare. He laughs when conditions demand tears; cries "wolf" to disguise his own character and hide his crimes; and curses when he should pray. Man lives on expectations, but has little to offer in return. He tries to master time, only to find that time will blow the dust which once spelled man from the palm of destiny.

His Spirit wanders among the stars, propounding

the possibility of his own adaptability on other worlds in a not so distant future. As yet he has not solved the secret of life within himself, let alone the bridging of space to far-away planets. Little does he suspect that time is non-existent, space unlimited, and that life and death have their conception only in him. He wants to live, but wills himself to die. He preserves his life with one thought and destroys it with another. If life begets only life, why does he worry about death? If acorns produce only oaks, what can the living seed in man produce but living man? If man must worship a God as the giver of life, why can he not worship Him through the medium of his own body as a temple, and keep that temple scrupulously clean?

At his leisure, man visits the zoo and marvels at the different forms and habits of life. I have often wondered whether the captives also marvel at the queer upstart, man, and his antics. Usually man is blissfully blind to things he ought to see. His sentiment is easily aroused, producing within himself all sorts of mental disorders. He has hallucinations and illusions, and his hysterics drive him toward destruction. He declares himself for peace, but plots wars as soon as he sees that his neighbor is human and vulnerable. He makes his own laws, disobeys them, and then resents punishment. He is contrary to everything within reason and possibility. He wishes for progress, but is himself a stumbling-block most of the time. There is no other animal on the face of the earth that is so conceited, revengeful, bigoted, arrogant, destructive, murderous, false, and faithless as man. He seems to have an uncanny faculty of absorbing bad tendencies from all other animals combined, and has had ever since he first evolved from fish to man,

If it is man's sacred contention that a God created him in His own image he certainly gives such a God no credit as far as spiritual qualities are concerned. It is quite unbelievable that a deity should waste his time creating a two-legged termite which would later bore him tremendously, annoy and disobey him, curse him, humiliate him before his spiritual host. Unless evolution provides man with an improved thinking apparatus, he will never learn to see God's face in his spiritual existence. Man has yet to learn that this universe does not rotate around man's ego and his many material desires. Neither will it yield to man its secrets easily and unchallenged. It is better to think of this earth as a sort of reformatory, a hell hole in creation, wherein all evil has been cast from other planets since time began. There is perhaps no other choice in redeeming one's Spirit or Soul than to live within a human beast — as a punishment — for a time, and, according to good or bad behavior, to be accepted or rejected once more. Few have had the rare and divine fortitude to attain a spiritual realm of existence while yet in their animal hides.

Man's greatest mistake has been the fact that he prefers to live contrary to natural laws. He eats and drinks most of what is most harmful to his health, thereby poisoning himself systematically. At the same time he bemoans the ailments he has brought upon himself. He swallows narcotics and alchohol, thus drugging his senses — which even normally are none too bright — and speeding his ever-decaying body closer to its ultimate destruction by way of self-inflicted torment. There is not another animal which would live an existence so utterly contrary to health, and to social and sex life, than the "crown of creation," the super animal, man. It is quite unthinkable that a horse should drink alcohol until his feet cave under him. No one has ever heard of a lion, eagle, or even a mouse, taking narcotics in order to receive an additional thrill. At feeding time they are not gluttons; neither do they diet themselves into skeletons. This sort of thing is practised only by thoughtless mankind. Today the female bears children not for the love of them, but because she is bribed into production. An animal will not succumb to such foolishness. Only in rare cases will an animal be so cannibalistic as to devour its own brood. Yet insurance money, ransom, or a grudge, are often sufficient provocation for the murder of children and adults.

Man, stripped of all his glory, repulsive in his nakedness, is merely stardust which has learned to breathe a mysterious composition giving it life. When once more reduced to matter, it will be blown into space or over the earth, and will formulate new, grotesque shapes capable of again breathing a chemical compound — air. For what divine or mysterious purpose is this endless cycle within an endless cosmos? To better man's spiritual conception of what is known as "the Father's house"? Or must man be led towards total annihilation because of his stupid attitude and waste of power? Shall the earth, which could have been the paradise promised to humans, become the tomb for an imbecilic and unworthy race which is too slow to absorb the Thought of truth and to act accordingly? Perhaps it is just as well either way. The earth will not stop rotating just because a horde of hijackers and parasites have ceased to exist and have made room for something more tangible, intelligent, and reasonable. It matters not in what shape new inhabitants may materialize, so long as the earth stops its rivers of blood which flow periodically from man-made slaughter houses.

## PIONEERS OF TOMORROW

WHEN man suspects and fears his fellow beings, he tries to safeguard his own interests with treaties, pacts, peace conferences, and alliances, so that he may secure a foothold over potential or imaginary enemies. Yet when his high pressure salesmanship has reached an irresistible force — or when all his efforts, logic, and reason have been stalemated — he disregards all secrecy and precaution, cancels all peaceful gestures, and runs to his arsenal for weapons, so that he may destroy, if possible, whatever stands in his path. The causes for such changes in attitude differ greatly. Sometimes it is a border line, a river, a religious or political alibi which "provoked" the conflict or war. Sometimes it is the mineral wealth within the earth which provides the excuse and brings out the ferocious beast in man, urging him to kill his unsuspecting neighbor, or to drive him from his territory. Competition for markets caused countless wars, and will cause more unless man begins to understand that treaties, pacts, and conferences breed only war, and war creates new alliances and treaties all over again. This endless cycle does humanity no good whatsoever, and nourishes fear, hatred, and contempt. The conquerer deems himself superior and beyond reproach, until he himself is conquered for possession of the halo with which he has surrounded himself.

Since all humans originated on this earth exclusively,

it matters little where one is born and educated. From earth, we materialize temporarily into existence, live but for only a comparative moment, and go back again into earth. Since all are entitled to all the wealth and health here on this planet, why should men fight among themselves for possession of a certain portion of soil? We are citizens of this earth and are entitled to all the considerations it has to offer. It is nonsense to believe that when a creature migrates into another territory, he becomes foreign, alien, and inferior. The sun gives light and warmth to all inhabitants of earth. A man born in Africa and going to another continent still remains a man; he does not have one foot on Martian soil and another here on earth. Therefore, he cannot possibly be an alien or a foreigner. Neither does his migration make him inferior. To be actually an "alien" one would have to come from another world. Perhaps it would be a good thing for us if "aliens" of that sort did come among us. It would automatically unite all earthlings, even those who seemingly canont keep away from one another's throats. An invasion of such aliens would make us all earth-conscious, and soon border lines would melt like ice in the sun, and leave all of us "world citizens." If the war-makers still felt like scrapping, in the event of such an invasion, they would not scrap among themselves, but would face such true alien creatures together.

What a break it would be for Alexander, if he lived today, to realize that there *are* more worlds to conquer! But why should humans wait to be attacked, unless it is the only thing which will bring them to their senses and make them realize that they are all equal? There is much ahead for humans if they would but listen to reason and science. Jesus, the son of a carpenter, did not live in the so-called scientific age, yet somehow he knew that there are many "mansions" in the Father's "house." With modern eyes or telescopes, men today are able to see for themselves what the Galilean teacher meant by the Father's house and its many, many mansions. He could not have seen them at that time with physical eyes, yet he knew that wherever the rays of beneficial solar fire would penetrate there would be light and warmth which, in its own queer way, would create shapes, growths, and intellects, alien to our own perhaps, but nevertheless live. "Blessed are they that have not seen, and yet have believed."

Certainly the Father would not have been justified in building a universe and in isolating the tiny creature, man, upon this earth just for the sake of mockery. Will man never learn that not this earth alone is his homestead, but that all within the cosmos cries out for exploration and possible colonization? There are enough worlds swimming in space to make men realize that fighting among themselves will not solve anything. If man must fight, then let him conquer space and make transportation between the planets his accomplishment. Let him mold his modern war machinery into space cruisers. Being a war hero is quite insignificant in comparison with pioneering into fields unknown with an objective of conquering space and establish themselves upon new worlds. Scientists from all over the globe must give their utmost, mentally and physically, in order to discover nature's secrets and to bring men to reason and make good world citizens out of them.

If man must expand, in order to take care of his own, then he must not do it at the expense of any of his fellow creatures, which in the end would injure the welfare of all concerned. Expansion must come first from within. A broad vision will carry man into territory as yet untouched by any man's foot. There is salvation and survival in directing oneself toward heaven, not in a religious sort of way, but in reality. One must travel heavenwards in order to see with mortal eyes the marvelous house and its many mansions which have been eternally in existence. What fascinating moments the first group of earthlings will experience when, looking into heaven, they recognize their home planet, from an alien world, shining like a diadem in the crown of that universal master organism! Will man recognize God's spiritual face and His nearness at such moments? Will he listen to that small voice and its glorious revelation that the new heaven and the new earth has always been waiting for him, but that stubborn resistance, superstition, and ignorance have kept him from it? Since thousands of years of constant warfare and strife have not solved man's problems, is it possible to believe that at last the human race has tired of this way and will now try a new and heavenly road, in order to preserve itself?

Does it matter just where one's bones may again be transformed into stardust, as long as they carried their owner to a distinct goal? Why has man not used his inventive genius for something really worth while? Life is cheap in peace time; it is worth nothing during periods of war; but it will become priceless when successful travel between worlds has been established. Almost the entire human race would depend upon the "Columbus of space" for instructions for possible migration. An entirely new industry would come into existence, eradicating a great deal of unemployment and misery. Surely people will follow such a discoverer rather than remain and listen to war-breeders and destructive Pied Pipers. In all likelihood they will, unless science sells out to evil forces, and they are destroyed completely, by their own creations.

(The Author is a member of the British Interplanetary Society, London, England, since March, 1946; and also a member of the United States Rocket Society, Inc., of Glen Ellyn, Illinois, since July, 1946.)

# FEAR — THE INVISIBLE RULER

It has been truly said that the gods are fearless and that humans may become godlike by the conquest of fear. Yet from the beginning man has submitted to this relentless foe and has subconsciously obeyed and even worshipped it. He has as yet found no lasting remedy for the chronic condition within the mind which allows fear to be master. Untold misery through all the ages can be traced to this invisible force; hideous tyrant that it is, it makes a total wreck of all who submit to it. As long as man has walked the earth, fear has somehow managed to be his faithful, unseen companion, and has hindered his progress and been an absolute nuisance to him.

A man's shadow, given him by light, and over which he has no control, may be easily compared with fear, the unnecessary evil, which follows him like a creature out of a nightmare for the rest of his days. Most spiritual advisers can do nothing to stop this deadly, poisonous, and destructive emotion within their fellow creatures. On the contrary, their twisted dogmas sometimes add to that fear. It is easy to get control, even of adults, by frightening them out of their wits with exaggerated bed-time stories.

During the World War soldiers were given stimulants, not to bring courage but to subdue fear. Others became heroes, not because they had courage, but because they were paralyzed with fear, and in that state committed unconscious and unbelievable feats of "heroism." To define fear, in its diversified manifestations, is next to impossible. To define Love, Life, or God is impossible also. Fear is universal; no man can honestly say that he is not, at times, plagued to a certain degree by that emotion. Our very existence is one of fear, from the cradle to the grave, and even beyond that. Why, nobody seems to know or to care. A world free of fear is almost unimaginable. It seems as though some men enjoy fearing one another, and even themselves. The character of man is shaped by his thinking processes, and whatever dominates his Spirit manifests during his living moments. Fear is contagious; it causes mass hysteria, panic, and fanaticism, which in turn cause wars, persecution, the spread of disease, and famine. But the moment fear does vanish from the mind, then reason and logic return. Fear seems to appear and to travel in cycles, paralyzing all thought, like a wild fire beyond control. But if humans had enough will power to fight that scared feeling and to counteract it, they might be able to banish fear at least temporarily, perhaps for good. Security has vanished from the earth, during the present war scare, and this fear exceeds avalanche proportion second only to the Biblical deluge. All habits can be broken, provided a sincere effort is made, and so it is with fear and worry. Man will never enjoy freedom unless he frees himself from fear. While he remains in its grasp, he is but half the "civilized" person he thinks himself to be. His true greatness depends entirely on how fast he releases himself from Demon "Fear."

Man should not worship in fear, now or ever. Precaution and preservation, however, have nothing to do with fear. To be fearless is not necessarily to be reckless. Animals know nothing of fear as humans do.

With them it is a matter of self-preservation that keeps them ever watchful for danger. The average human often disregards all caution and good judgment, and ignores real danger — not because he is unafraid, but to challenge danger and to invite the eventual consequences. There are others who think that by breaking all ties with this world they will escape damnation and punishment in the "next." Fear of the "hereafter" has crippled the thinking apparatus of a good many people. That's why we still have cloisters and monasteries filled with the living dead who are driven mad by fear, self-torment, and self pity, because they cling to the conviction that by denying themselves the worth-while things of life they may be spared eternal torment. In a mentally and physically sick body, there is no room for brilliant thoughts. By surrounding themselves with gloom, weird ceremonies, and concentrating on death alone, the inmates of cloisters and monasteries commit premeditated suicide, and benefit no one but the undertaker. Jesus never demanded such a silly and useless practise from anybody. Spiritual elevation, not fear-inspired, intentional degradation, was the original program of the early Christians.

Why is man so much concerned about a heaven in which to live, when all he does here is to make earth a constant hell-fire? It would not take him very long to transform his imaginary "heaven" also into a place of damnation. The meaning of heaven is very much misunderstood. Man points to the sky and imagines that heaven will be found somewhere in the direction of the Milky Way, all because he is afraid to accept his heaven on earth. "On earth, as it is in heaven" is a very nice prayer, but men are afraid to answer their own wants and to bring about a heaven on earth. No, they leave it among the stars to be enjoyed "in the sweet bye and bye." Man is like that. What little happiness he has he destroys, or else removes it far out of reach and admires it from a distance. He could have everlasting peace, but he much prefers war once in a while. After he has had his play with guns and soldiers and is quite nauseated by the stench of blood and decaying bones, peace looks good again, because he fears that nobody may be left to rebuild and to populate cities and towns if war is continued indefinitely.

The weather is another pet worry of his. It is never quite right. He is afraid of too much rain, snow, sun, and wind, or perhaps of too little. As far as the weather is concerned, just try to make it right, and you have succeeded in making it wrong, according to man.

There would have been little or no progress had it not been for a few fearless ones who often faced situations worse than death. Columbus, Magellan, Gallileo, Newton, Copernicus, Gutenberg, Pasteur, Roentgen, Zeppelin, Ford, are men who have helped to improve conditions and the general conception of the relation of this earth to the cosmic scheme. Others will come, will fearlessly make use of knowledge left to them, and will alter conditions for the better, educate the ignorant and the mentally slow, thus wiping out the evil remnant of man's arch enemy, fear. Their weapon, formulated by modern spiritual alchemy, as yet not fully understood, will be Psycho —Truth —Radiation.

## LIVE ACCORDING TO NATURE AND BE HEALTHY!

"And God said, Behold, I have given you every herb [vegetable] bearing seed, which is upon the face of all the earth, and every tree, in the which is the fruit of a tree yielding seed: to you it shall be for meat." — Genesis 1:29.

"For I have no pleasure in the death of him that dieth, saith the Lord God: wherefore turn yourselves, and live ye." — Ezekiel 18:32.

This message is not entirely new but has been rediscovered, revitalized, and streamlined. The simple truth will remain true wherever and whenever applied; the time element has little to do with it. Man was never meant to be a devourer of killed animals in order to nourish his body. By eating the dead meat of animals, man remains carnivorous, cannibalistic, and beastly. Today, since the discovery of vitamines in grain and vegetables, and its application as nourishment, man may live without meat and yet have more strength, vitality, and alertness of mind than he ever had before. He will thus return to nature, of which he is a product, and by obeying God's law he shall truly live. People kill themselves slowly when they allow ill-chosen food to enter their stomachs. They truly dig their graves with their own teeth. But it need not be so. For God told man what to eat in order to live, because he is the God of the living and has no interest in the dead. The mighty elephant, he who knows not his own strength, as well as the gorilla, are vegetarians by choice. It is not easy to break a habit, especially a habit of eating steaks and chops. But if man turns about in this respect, he will have less disease, more joy in living, and a keen mind in a healthy body. Then by all means break the old habit and begin a pleasant, correct and scientific one. Turn yourselves and live!

All raw vegetables, with their living protoplasm brought into existence by vegetable blood, when eaten raw, live in the stomach and intestines, where a chemical change permits their entrance into the blood stream. Cooked vegetables become waste matter, worthless except for the water in which they have been cooked. This sterilized extract makes a valuable food drink which purifies the blood and gives resistance and rejuvenation to the body. The water of all cooked vegetables is medicine for the complex digestive system, because its vital juices help the colon to eliminate its waste matter in a painless, effective, natural manner. The mysterious effect of the vegetable food drink tonic will give a person health and life if taken as often as possible. Chilled vegetable water makes an excellent drink before breakfast. Cultivated vegetables are within the reach of all classes of humans, especially here in America. Therefore, any individual may enjoy the benefits of nature's medicine chest if he wishes.

Nature's first law for humans, as recorded by ancient and mystic wisdom, is to be vegetarians. Meat and blood of killed animals were never meant for food. The gradual abstinence from all flesh food is essential to a change in diet. The meat of pork in any form must remain taboo. Abstain from eating the meat of crustacea when on a strict two months' vegetable diet. Drink no coffee, tea, cocoa; take no drugs or patent medicine when on this diet. A warm bath twice a week is sufficient. Excessive bathing is dangerous to health. Take deep breaths. These simple instructions are most effective during spring and autumn, when one's blood goes through a natural adjustment to climatic conditions. It should be adhered to for at least two months, during which time excessive smoking must be avoided.

Fill your mind with positive, creative thoughts, thus inviting into the body a spiritual force-vibration with every breath you take. See yourself as healthy, possessed of great vitality, filled with personal magnetism, and the power to accomplish great things.

By abstaining from fleshy substances like meat one can eat more food containing the necessary "building blocks" of health which are found in vitamines. According to modern food science, vitamines and their effects upon the human body, are classified as follows:

Vitamine A: Tomatoes, carrots, kale, spinach, turnips. Promotes growth, affords resistance to infection, and increases longevity.

Vitamine B: Tomatoes, green peas, green string beans, soy beans, asparagus, carrots, spinach. Promotes growth, appetite, stability.

Vitamine C: Tomatoes, green peas, raw cabbage, green peppers, parsley. Promotes growth; protects bone from decay.

Vitamine D: Halibut and cod oils, egg yolk, milk. Builds sound bone and teeth; prevents rickets.

Vitamine G: Spinach, kale, carrots, asparagus. Promotes growth; prevents pellagra.

### Live According To Nature and Be Healthy!

A strictly vegetarian diet, for those who sincerely desire good health, is given here with choice variation:

1. Oatmeal, cornflakes, adding wheat germ.
2. Fresh fruits of any kind, prepared in ways you enjoy: stewed apricots, prunes, or baked apples (avoid white sugar).
3. Celery, parsley, lettuce, dandelions, watercress.
4. Turnips, carrots, baked potato, sweet potato.
5. Green peas, lima beans.
6. Rice, corn on the cob, cauliflower, string beans, broccoli, asparagus, spinach.
7. Milk, pot cheese.
8. Avoid vinegar in salads and food preparations.
9. Grape fruit, oranges, pears, pineapple.
10. Vegetable water with the exception of potato water.
11. Honey, maple syrup, butter, marmalade.
12. Whole wheat bread, pumpernickel.

*Man's immortal spiritual units*
*Have free communion with the*
*Living Spirit of the universe,*
*Glorifying a message of a cosmic*
*Oneness within all in the flesh.*

## SYMBOLIC SUN WORSHIP

THERE is a striking resemblance between the ancient sun worship and idolatry — so fervently practised by the Egyptians — and the religion of Jews and Christians. It looks as though the leaders of the sons of Abraham adopted the teachings of the Egyptian priests when they adopted the name "Israel" and established themselves for the first time in history as a distinct race. Their leader Moses, who as an infant was found and adopted by an Egyptian princess, took it up himself to liberate his people from bondage and promised them territory and nationality. He called them the Children of Israel, which typifies a conglomeration of both faiths. By comparing the name Israel with the Egyptian name of Isis-Ra-Ba, one finds that — with the exception of the last syllable "el" in Israel, which is abbreviated from "Emanuel," or "God with us" — the similarity among the Egyptian, Jewish, and Christian religions is not by any means coincidental, as far as the doctrine of a divine trinity is concerned. As an outward symbol, Egypt has the triangular-shaped pyramids; whereas the Israelite has two interlocked triangles made into a star symbol.

Sun worship penetrated the land of Israel in Ezekiel's time, when he saw in a vision, according to Ezekiel 8:16, "At the door of the temple of the Lord, and their faces towards the east; and they worshipped the sun towards the east." Christians have, unintentionally perhaps, named three days after celestial bodies: the sun (Sunday), the moon (Monday), and the planet Saturnus (Saturday) which were known to the astrologers of Egypt without the aid of a telescope. It is surprising to notice that the Atlantians — who worshipped the "Eternal Light," or the living source of power and knowledge hidden within the nucleus of spiritual light — also were builders of pyramids. The civilization of Atlantis — that first continent known to have been inhabited by human beings — far surpassed our present one in art and science. There is little doubt that, before the submersion of Atlantis took place, the priests planned excursions to what is now known as Egypt and Central America, in order that they might continue their civilization there. The Mayan and the Egyptian forms of civilization, art, architecture, and worship are identical, and probably originated from the sunken but not forgotten Atlantis. What happened to the priests of this intelligent race of humans still remains a mystery; but much will be known to the world when submarines locate the hidden temples of a slowly rising continent. Science will decipher the carvings, inscribed by priests and wise men of that time, on tablets and slates, and we will gain knowledge — let us hope superior to our own. The worship of eternal spiritual light — which alone can illuminate the Soul of man — outlasts time itself and witnesses that it is not man-made religion but rather an eternal radiation, dominating this planet and the entire cosmos.

Aryan ancestors of the European and American people — Mayan, Aztecs, Incas — were sun worshippers. It is recorded in history that in ancient times there lived a race of Aryans, in the mountain lands of

Central Asia, who spoke a language not Sanskrit, Greek, or German, but a dialect of all three. These people were advanced to a state of agricultural civilization, and they recognized the bonds of blood and marriage. They worshipped nature. The sun was not merely a luminary, but creator, ruler, and savior. Branches of this Aryan race migrated to the east and west. One founded the Persian kingdom, another the Greek nation; a third went to Italy and is responsible for imperial Rome. England reveals Aryan descendancy. Germany also is peopled by Aryans. Other bands of Aryans found their way through the passes of the Himalayas into Punjab, to rule as Brahmins over India. They are twelve names given to the sun in the form of salutations, by the worshippers in India. They are:

1. Mitra, friend of all.
2. Ravi, praised by all.
3. Surya, director or stimulator.
4. Bhanu, giving lustre or beauty.
5. Khaga, stimulator of the senses.
6. Pooshan, nourisher.
7. Hiranyagarbha, possessing power to develop energy and vitality.
8. Marichi, destroyer of disease.
9. Aditya, attractor.
10. Savitri, begetter.
11. Arka, fit to be revered.
12. Bhaskara, refulgent.

Christians all over the earth celebrate the 25th of December as the birthday of Jesus the Christ. But He was never born on that day. The 25th of December was originally set aside by the so-called pagans as a day of rejoicing over the fact that the sun and earth were coming into exact conjunction, allowing the sun's rays to give light and warmth at a rate of three minutes with each additional day after December 25th. The early Christians, however, chose that day as a protection against raids and molestations from followers of other faiths, seeing that they were then quite occupied with sun worship. So up to this day, Christians are in full sympathy with the principle of life-giving and sustaining forces generated by sun-rays, even though it has been clothed quite carefully with a man-made religious atmosphere ever since.

Symbol of Divine Trinity, as first used in Egypt.
Isis — Egyptian goddess.
Ra — Egyptian sun god.
Ba — Bird spirit of man.

The children of
Is — ra — el.
Isis — Egyptian goddess.
Ra — Egyptian sun god.
El — Emanuel (God with us).

## ATOMIC ATTRACTION, CONCENTRATION, AND ADJUSTMENT

THOUGHT frequency creates sound vibrations not audible to human ears. The super sensitive cosmic radiation is affected, permitting these vibrations to travel into the desired, hoped for, prayed for direction, and returning it, boomerang-like, to its originator with astounding results. Thus cosmic radiation reaches out into the center of the atomic structure to select desired matter or to change it into definite organic or inorganic objects, according to the strength and persistence of the Thought frequency sender. A sort of white magic takes place, whereby spiritual Thought is utilized to transform seemingly invisible matter, atomic in its origin, into recognizable possibilities. It is thus that the living, atomic matter employs Thought to perform the miracle of transmuting matter and creating entirely new shapes — by pulling away atomic matter, magnet-like, from a hostile cosmos, this action being set into motion by the output of active Thought frequency. A sort of atom splitting — on a limited scale — seems to be taking place in all of us, all the time, and for a definite purpose. A well-balanced output of force, emitted through the medium of Thought frequency, draws unknown amounts of cosmic power toward its sender. This power is waiting for proper absorption within the center of the living atom, and will transform the individual and give him health, wealth, wisdom, and power.

## Atomic Attraction, Concentration, & Adjustment

Cosmic interference upon the channels of atomic attraction is more or less responsible for sudden changes concerning the success, failure, health, sickness, and moods of the individual. Materialization and disappearance are, in all probability, caused by light and sound effects upon matter; and they demand atomic adjustment of both the inert and animated matter. Darkness is absence of light; thus it will not register on normal optic nerves. Objects become invisible not for lack of existence but because of the change which the atomic structure undergoes. The same phenomenon occurs when sound becomes inaudible to the ear — when stepped up to a high pitch, matter and atomic composition is affected to a degree where the superstitious alchemist may well believe in black magic! Objects placed behind a powerful glare of light are not recognizable — in fact, they often seem to disappear from view. Light thus plays tricks and causes illusions and hallucinations; it produces phantoms because of the altered atomic force and because of its electronic concentration upon both animate and inanimate objects. Where there is seemingly nothing in existence, atoms concentrate and attract, forming objects and conditions to dazzle the human senses (Fata morgana), a display of natural magic on a grand scale, proving to perplexed and fearful humans that not always does seeing mean believing — not in a world where little atoms play a rather independent part, as far as their adaptability to cosmic changes is concerned.

## SPIRITUAL THOUGHT RENAISSANCE

In order to counteract successfully the evil thought of hate which results in war, one must have an antidote. Good will and peace are the opposites of war, which can and must be abolished. Strong and disciplined concentration on peace will eject war mongering and other evil propaganda from the mind of man. In order to accomplish this, man must learn that his destiny on this earth has little to do with his physical appearance, and everything to do with the thoughts which mold and direct his inner man. He must accept the fact that we are all humans, products of mother earth, and that when we behave contrary to the laws of nature we must suffer the consequences. We bring evil upon ourselves, and should not blame our neighbors for our own shortcomings. It is absolutely necessary to be strictly honest with oneself, and to direct one's thought first and last toward good will for all men on this earth. Such spiritual Thought radiation can come only from within; it must be combined with the sincere wish to understand the problems confronting our fellow creatures. It is not given to man to know and to understand all things, but he should seek to follow to the best of his ability when those more intelligent than he clear the way for a better and safer future, a more unselfish and harmonious mode of living.

It will be necessary, some day, to let scientists guide the human race, if men wish to survive at all. We should entrust our fate, and that of generations to come, to psychic and scientific individuals who fight destructive forces. In my humble opinion, I think it is high time to choose between constructive and destructive forces; and if we must do some constructive fighting, let it be a war against war and evil propaganda. We came to this earth to live, not to die like animals, slaughtered on the so-called "field of honor," for the benefit of a certain evil minority. The aim of man is life, laughter, and the perpetuation of his own kind. This cannot be accomplished through a medium of periodical destruction and annihiliation as gruesome as war. There is no profit, spiritual or material, in any war; there is only a harvest of tomb stones, cripples, orphans, taxation, and rivers of tears and regret. We want to live in peace with everyone on this planet. Those still clinging to ancient dogmas and superstitions must be educated to realize the meaning of world citizenship, and of a world alliance guided by mentally and scientifically superior men. If we help, even in our little way, to outlaw conflicts and wars, and thus bring about a true and safe dawn of civilization, our ideals will not be lost among the incoming generation. They will say that we used inspired Thoughts at the right time and in the right place. They will say that their fathers took it upon themselves to ban hell forever from this earth and to replace it with heaven on earth for all of us.

## SPIRITUAL CONCEPT AND MATERIALIZATION

WHAT great amazement it would cause if a fleet of space cruisers should successfully land on this earth a cargo of weird creatures from another world! Could the mind of the average Twentieth Century human understand the purpose of such an adventure by alien creatures? Could it understand their far superior scientific findings, weapons, modes of travel and communication, their combat of disease, and methods of warfare? Is it not likely that, because of their foreign "magic," we might consider them "gods from heaven?" Were not Columbus and his seafaring crew at first worshipped as beings from another world, until they were found to be just as mortal as the native Caribs? Cortez and his greedy, gold-hungry companions were accepted as white gods by superstitious Montezuma and his Aztecs. The primitive and semi-civilized tribes had never heard or seen anything superior to their own kind of living, and when these miracle-working aliens appeared, it was natural that their fear and superstition drenched minds should worship them.

Sacrifices in the form of gifts, combined with weird rituals, for the purpose of impressing and gaining favor from the "gods," have been practised ever since the first tribal god Jehovah made it clear to Abraham that he wished to be obeyed and worshipped. God made it clear that He and no one else has a final claim to this earth, its inhabitants, its wealth and welfare as stated in Exodus 34:13, 14: "But ye the Israelites shall destroy their altars, break their images, and cut down their groves: For thou shalt worship no other god: for the Lord, whose name is Jealous, is a jealous God:" For obedience of all laws given to Moses, this self-appointed God promised protection against any other tribe and their beliefs, together with destruction to any opposition which might hamper the desire to rule his selected ones. With truly modern, superior, unearthly weapons and methods this God Jehovah overawed the Israelites from the very beginning. His appearance to Moses on Mount Sinai is a colossal, phenomenal spectacle, and as seen from the modern viewpoint, must have been done with the aid of a rocketship or space sphere, which accounts for the noise, smoke, and firey blasts of rocket propulsion, as stated in the simple language of Exodus 19:16–20:

*16. And it came to pass on the third day, in the morning, that there were thunders and lightnings, and a thick cloud upon the mount, and the voice of the trumpet exceeding loud so that all the people that was in the camp trembled.*
*17. And Moses brought forth the people out of the camp to meet with God; and they stood at the nether part of the mount.*
*18. And mount Sinai was altogether on a smoke, because the LORD descended upon it in fire: and the smoke thereof ascended as the smoke of a furnace, and the whole mount quaked greatly.*
*19. And when the voice of the trumpet sounded long, and waxed louder and louder, Moses spake, and God answered him by a voice.*
*20. And the LORD came down upon mount Sinai, on the top of the mount: and the LORD called Moses up to the top of the mount; and Moses went up.*

Superior creatures and experts on interplanetary

travel must account for the stories of winged angels, having good intentions toward man. Yet strange to say, this same God has forbidden certain vital knowledge regarding the formulas which preserve the body from disease, death, decay, as told in Genesis 3: 22–24:

22. *"And the LORD God said, Behold, the man is become as one of us, to know good and evil: and now, lest he put forth his hand, and take also of the tree of life, and eat, and live for ever:*
23. *Therefore the LORD God sent him forth from the garden of Eden to till the ground from whence he was taken.*
24. *So he drove out the man; and he placed at the east of the garden of Eden, cherubims, and a flaming sword which turned every way, to keep the way of the tree of life.*

In order to prevent man from becoming eternal and like a god, an officer with a flaming sword —in modern terms, a Ray pistol issuing flame — was placed near the "Fountain of Youth," the "Tree of Life," by use of which man could materialize anywhere at any time, and disappear at will. Further on, we see that the sons of God, these mysterious space travelers from far-off planets, took earth females as wives, and created new lives, god-men, giants. Genesis 6:1–4 states clearly that the blood of the gods crossed the blood of earthlings, and thus a certain percentage of them became more or less sons of gods themselves, originated by the divine symbol of the cross, representing union, fusion of blood of one with another. Genesis 6:

1. *And it came to pass, when men began to multiply on the face of the earth, and daughters were born unto them.*
2. *That the sons of God saw the daughters of men*

## Spiritual Concept and Materialization 103

that they were fair; and they took them wives of all which they chose.

3. And the LORD said, My Spirit shall not always strive with man, for that he also is flesh: yet his days shall be an hundred and twenty years.

4. There were giants in the earth in those days; and also after that, when the sons of God came in unto the daughters of men, and they bare children to them, the same became mighty men, which were of old, men of renown.

It will please the Father to have obedient children — taking more and more after Him and losing much of their animal nature — who will in due time understand the mighty plan to inherit and to inhabit other planets within the universe. It will repay Him for all the effort and humiliation endured in trying to rear and to educate mere animals, and to bring them to a higher level of existence. If the gods wish to rule over us, they are certainly entitled to do it, as long as the sons of men cannot duplicate all their feats of magic, cannot travel to other worlds, cannot make themselves invisible, cannot live indefinitely. Man wishes to be ruled, especially by something or someone mystifying and supernatural. So the gods answer their prayer, and man may well have faith in an invisible and intelligent power, rather than in idols carved out of gold, ivory, or wood, representing men, beasts or trees. How deeply we still believe in our forefathers' superstitious conceptions depends on our mental impressions and reactions. If mental evolution within the creature will permit a super race to dominate this planet, and if science — coldly calculating but truly divine — is the reception committee to welcome space travelers — let us say from Mars — then of course superstition will receive a sound thrashing — to the dismay of religious profiteers — when "men from Mars" are announced, and not "gods from Mars." To welcome them is, in my opinion, more sensible, tolerant, and acceptable than to start a crusade against the "invaders" because they do not bring a crucifix, holy water, and incense. It would be extremely wise to find out just how much we can learn from these outsiders before we run to the arsenal and make hostile enemies of creatures with perhaps good intentions. When treated with respect and tact, creatures who are so learned as to know about gravity and space travel would certainly not behave like the Spanish conquistadore Pizarro, Cortez, or even Columbus. If we should challenge them to war, we would probably come out second best, because our methods of warfare would probably be merely child's play to them.

Those ingenious, large-eyed creatures, with small hands, who long ago gave up the spoken and written language and use only symbols and telepathy for communication, may well teach man a thing or two on the point of a disintegration ray, instead of a schoolmaster's hickory stick. If we of today did not find it necessary as yet to construct space fleets to carry the true "sons of God" away from earth, then it is high time that the Revelation of St. John should bring us the Prince of Peace out of Heaven, even if he has to ride a rocket ship in order to get here. There are enough mansions (planets) floating in the universe, or the Father's house, that each of us could settle on one of them, with the aid of a space ship of his own, and start his own kind of "God business," provided the inhabitants would accept it. At any rate, he could still be an honored, universal scientist, wherever he landed.

"The works that I do, ye shall do also" was a promise of a much misunderstood spiritual teacher. When he ascended towards heaven, it was an example for us to do the same, in a quite material sort of way. Airplanes have already put wings onto men, but this is insignificant as long as gravity and mother earth still pull adventurous rascals back to her bosom. Sometimes I wonder if the gods enjoy themselves watching us and our vain attempts to duplicate their greater magic without first consulting them in spirit. As far as Jehovah God is concerned, much of his mysticism can be explained, together with his purpose, except that he has remained an enigma as far as his features are concerned. For reasons of his own, no one shall see his face and live; not even his confederate Moses was allowed such a privilege. Perhaps a shield of radium is covering his immune features, so powerful and so destructive to us mortals that its radiation instantly kills when it is contacted. Radio, television, technicolor in movies, newsprint, loud speakers, artificial lightning, the splitting of atoms in cyclotrons, restoration of sight, raising the dead, artificial lung, X-ray, anesthesia, smoke screen, explosives, germ warfare, poison gas, flame throwers, bombing planes, submarines, mines, tanks, fire from heaven, the atom bomb, surgery, gland transplantation, rubber, electricity, telephone, cable, radium, modern Babylonian towers, steamships, Diesel motors, subway, bridges, telescopes, microscopes — all are witnesses of a successful, spiritually guided animal who tries to understand the mysterious code whispered to him during blissful meditation, through the medium of Thought. Such is the son of man, trying to become the true son of God, in order to inherit the universe with all its planets, as a reward for obedience, or doomed to be exterminated from the earth for disobeying a far superior power and intelligence within the cosmos. Man takes much for granted, even from the gods. A sign of some significance and magnitude would perhaps convince him of what he cannot otherwise grasp. Yet would he be prepared for the unusual, the supernatural? If such a phenomenon did not kill him outright, the shock might make him an invalid, would probably leave him a mental derelict. Not everyone can become a Moses, a Joan of Arc, a Mohamet, a Buddha, or even an Attila who called himself "the scourge of God." Or, in modern language —not every mortal has the psychic inner vision to sense or to know that power has been granted for the purpose of transmitting a personal trend of Thought upon others, yet still to remain within the frame of God-consciousness. Even dictators have a religious sort of faith as far as their aims are concerned. They would not exist at all without such a faith. The world would not have known Alexander, Caesar, Genghis Khan, or Napoleon, except for the results of the ambitions to which they gladly and faithfully subscribed their bodies and Souls.

Of faith, this strange, powerful emotion, it is said in Matthew 17:

18. *And Jesus rebuked the devil, and he departed out of him; and the child was cured from that very hour.*
19. *Then came the disciples to Jesus apart, and said, Why could not we cast him out?*
20. *And Jesus said unto them, Because of your unbelief; for verily I say unto you, If ye have faith as a grain of mustard seed, ye shall say unto this mountain, Remove hence to yonder place, and it shall remove; and nothing shall be impossible unto you.*

The **spiritual spark, called** memory, subconsciously betraying hereditary conception of superiors from heaven as conceived by men on earth, finds its outlet in faith as a final fusion of forces, and literally lifts man from one planet toward another, giving him a freedom never known before, to exist in matter somewhere, as a reward for faith, shaping his destiny and perpetuation as the true son of the gods.

## SYMBOLIC LANGUAGE

Language is a conveyor of ideas. Unless the reader has a keen mind, alert to detect the unwritten and invisible suggestions, much of the value of language is lost. Especially in the Bible do we find hidden truths in parables and symbolic suggestions. This reading between the lines of cold type is of real value and is a gift to individuals, to clarify spiritual meanings which are clerely hidden within an array of symbols, so that the average reader is not aware of the message within a message. Symbolic or code language was used by Egyptian priests in order to abbreviate as much as possible the spoken language of their day and yet to retain the value and meaning for the ages to come; and their messages were artfully preserved in stone. We of today are imitating the ancient symbolic sort of language known only to the initiate, or obtained after much study on the various subjects. I wish to quote a few examples of what was meant by symbol language thousands of years ago, also to tell how this knowledge has been kept alive to this day by a changing priest-class, in order that they keep well informed of coming events, and yet at the same time keep the common man at a respectable distance, thus retaining a worship of intelligence which only the material-minded wishes to perpetuate, and which finds its best and most profitable outlet in the various brands of man-made religions.

*Moses*, named by an Egyptian princess, using the symbol language of the priest-class and their viewpoint in relation to the sun and planetary vibrations on life as we know it.

*Mars* — Planet of War.
*Osiris* — Egyptian god of the dead.
*Sun* — Giver of life.
*Earth* — Planet or origin.
*Saturn* — Planet.

By using the first letter of the above words, you will get the symbolic name of *Moses*.

*Jesus*, named in Isaiah 12:14, long before His birth, and later in St. Luke 1:31, with the knowledge of Egyptian symbol language, understanding planetary vibrations as a stimulus on human behavior, thus proclaiming Jesus as the Messiah, restoring an ancient faith in natural forces, bringing man back to the divine laws of nature. "If ye had known me [Jesus or the influence of the planets], ye should have known my Father (Universe) also," said the Galilean teacher. for "In my Father's house [Universe] are many mansions [planets]."

*Jupiter* — Biggest planet.
*Earth* — Planet of origin.
*Sun* — Giver of life.
*Uranus* — Planet of psychic powers.
*Saturn* — Planet.

By using the first letter of above words, you will get the symbolic name and meaning of *Jesus*.

The ancient city of *Rome* is also named after using Egyptian symbol language.

*Ra* — Sun god of the Egyptians.
*Osiris* — Egyptian god of the dead.

*Mars* — Planet of war.
*Earth* — Planet of origin.

The word *radio* or the voice of God, and the word *radium* or the ray of God, betray the symbolic origin of ancient Egypt. Ra was the sun god of Egypt, and Dio means God in the land of the inventor Marconi.

The symbolic meaning of the word *Israel* given to the Jews betrays Egyptian influence, when we take into consideration the long period of time which lapsed before the exodus, when the Jews were under Egyptian rule; the spiritual influence left its mark, in the term; the "children of Israel," which is a conglomeration of both Egyptian and Jewish tribal faith in spiritual phenomena.

*Is* — Isis, Egyptian goddess of the moon.
*ra* — Ra, sun god of the Egyptians.
*el* — Emanuel, Jewish faith in invisible God.

A modern revival of symbolic language is here today; for example: WPA, TWA, CCC, AAA, NBC, U.S.A., showing a spiritual renaissance of true Egyptian knowledge, a spirit reborn into modern age bodies, as a forerunner of the spiritual leadership of the symbolic meaning incorporated in the name Jesus.

## NOVUS ORDO SECLORUM
### The "New Order of Ages"

COMING events cast their shadows before. So did the prophesy connecting the pyramid of Gizeh, Egypt, foretell the conditions prior to *novus ordo seclorum*, or the new order of ages, as seen by the psychic priestclass of Egypt, whose records are revealed in Bible passages by those fortunate enough to have been instructed by Egyptian astrologers and its priestclass. We of today are in the advent stage of changes so startling, swift, and perplexing that conditions may well be likened to the "end of the world" and its ways to which we have been accustomed till now, ushering in a truly new order of ages and things alien to all of us. Changes of such gigantic proportions that it will take nothing less than the planets themselves to set the stage — with their powerful influence and radiation on earth — to bring about the Aquarian ruled section of the Zodiac, together with its humanitarian tendencies, science, and progress, into its rightful position for the benefit of all mankind and for all generations to come. I wish to quote several interesting passages saturated with the wisdom of a psychic few living in the past, looking into the future with that uncanny sense and perception of the spiritual inner eye, seeing and believing in conditions truly foreign and often sinister, as far as their physical environment was concerned. I also wish to give the proper significance and translation to these puzzling presentations of minds radiated with that divine spark, so necessary for advancement of a race and civilization.

*And great earthquakes shall be in divers places, and famines, and pestilences; and fearful sights and great signs shall there be from heaven.* — Luke 21:11.

Earthquakes, floods, hurricanes, meteorites, have struck terror into the hearts of humans living here and abroad, in recent years, with an appalling loss of life and property.

*And there shall be signs in the sun, and in the moon, and in the stars; and upon the earth distress of nations, with perplexity; the sea and the waves roaring;*
*Men's hearts failing them for fear, and for looking after those things which are coming on the earth: for the powers of heaven shall be shaken.* —Luke 21:25, 26.

1938 – 1939: Sunspots of enormous dimensions are turning toward the earth. 1939: Four planets, Jupiter, Saturn, Uranus, and Mars are bringing their radiation and planetary influence into play upon the earth, all at once and from one direction. 1939: The irregular course of the moon has been confirmed by the report made by Dr. H. Spencer Jones, astronomer at London, England. He states that the departure of the moon from its known mathematical course continues to increase and is now greater than at any time in the past two hundred and fifty years; furthermore, that no reason for this strange deflection is known. Is this phenomenon just another certain "sign" in accordance with the prophesy in verses 25 and 26, ushering in the new order of ages? 1938 – 1939: Fear, caused by the war of nerves, has gripped mankind in anticipation of the coming results caused by the "war of nerves." It has been admitted in medical centers that heart disease and heart failure among humans have increased to alarming proportion during the last few years.

*And then they shall see the Son of man coming in a cloud with power and great glory.*
*And when these things begin to come to pass, then look up, and lift up your heads; for your redemption draweth nigh.* — Luke 21:27, 28.

1939: Who is this "Son of man" appearing to be flying in the clouds? The superiority of modern air warfare in its origin went without question to Hitler's Germany. Was he the "Son of man" flying with his armada of airplanes through clouds, with power and great glory?

*And then shall appear the sign of the Son of man, in heaven: and then shall all the tribes of the earth mourn . . .* — Matthew 24:30.

His "sign," the swastika, has caused untold mourning amongst the tribes on earth. Hitler's talisman, the swastika, a celestial symbol, was revered in India three thousand years before Christianity, and back even into prehistoric times. It has been looked upon, like a wheel, as a symbol of solar energy, representing good fortune. It is based on the Sanskrit world meaning "it is well."

*Behold he cometh with clouds; and every eye shall see him, and they also which pierced him, and all kindred of the earth shall wail because of him.* — Rev. 1:7.
*Think not that I am come to send peace on earth: I came not to send peace, but a sword.* — Matt. 19:34.

Was the "sword" mentioned above Hitler? Are the planets grouped closely to earth, spelling out the spiritual coming of *Jesus*, when the letters are placed in the following formation: Jupiter, Earth, Sun, Uranus, Saturn? It certainly looks as if the nearness of Mars has caused peace to flee the earth and bring a "sword" instead. It is significant to note in verses 27 and 28, and in Matthew 24: 30 that nothing has been said about a coming of the "Son of God," but the coming of the "Son of man."

Taking into consideration all the other signs given, by which we should recognize the end of the old and the coming of the new order of ages, makes me feel that the phenomenal rise of Hitler was no mere coincident. Hitler, the "sword," has caused distress and perplexity to the leaders of nations on earth. Especially during World War II when Hitler had power over the destiny of such nations that were in direct contact with the "sword." "All kindred of the earth shall wail because of him" [the Son of man], showed clearly the startling sentiment of unpopularity and resentment against this man Hitler and his attempts to bring about changes on the earth so swift, revolutionary, and gigantic in dimension that for a while they heralded the "end of the world" for those who opposed the new order of things in connection with spiritual leadership, changing old dogmas and faith. There is hardly a person on the whole of the earth who has not at one time or another heard or seen Hitler, either by radio or by moving picture, another certain clue by which we of today should recognize the fulfillment of Revelation 1:7, where it is stated that every eye shall see him (the Son of man) whom I regard as no one else but Hitler.

The importance of radio for propaganda purposes and as an instrument of lightning-swift communication between countries at war or peace, has truly become the voice of God, invisible power, leaving its sound effects upon the minds of humans, so they may choose which road they should follow — a road leading toward a new order of ages, or one leading toward the annihiliation of humans. Will people of today make the colossal blunder of misusing power, unlike a race of people long since extinct from their home continent Atlantis, now submerged beneath the unruly waves of the Atlantic Ocean, with only a shattered remnant escaping to their colonial possession known today as Egypt; or will the advance stages of the new order be recognized by us today and preparation for adjustment be made by all the tribes of earth, thus receiving the new dawn of civilization, a sort of Goetterdaemmerung, seen in the spiritual light of those who prophesied conditions confronting all of us, thousands of years ago?

## THE CHILDREN OF "HEAVEN AND EARTH"

When comparing the mythology of earth people living apart from one another over great distances, as in this instance the Polynesians and the so-called "children of Israel," it is astounding to observe the similarity of thought as far as the union of heavenly creatures with earthlings is concerned. For futher comparison on this vital subject, I wish to quote from the story in the Bible to substantiate my claim; and after that I shall give the Polynesian version of the same subject, as taken from the *Guide to Mythology*, by Helen A. Clarke, a book edited in 1908.

*And it came to pass, when men began to multiply on the face of the earth, and daughters were born unto them,*
*That the sons of God saw the daughters of men that they were fair; and they took them wives of all which they chose.*
*And the* LORD *said, My spirit shall not always strive with men, for he that also is flesh; yet his days shall be a hundred and twenty years.*
*There were giants in the earth in those days; and also after that, when the sons of God came in unto the daughters of men, and they bare children to them, the same became mighty men and which were of old, men of renown.* — Genesis 6:1-4. (Origin of kings and royalty as the result of union of heaven and earth creatures.)

Now for the Polynesian version concerning the union of creatures of flesh (super scientists) coming from heaven or space, with the native creatures found on earth, thus becoming the children of heaven and earth:

## The Children of "Heaven and Earth"

*Men had but one pair of primitive ancestors; they sprang from the vast heaven that exists above us, and from the earth which lies beneath us. According to the tradition of our race, rangi and papa, or heaven and earth, were the sources from which in the beginning, all things originated. Darkness then rested upon the earth, and they still clave together, for they had not yet been rent apart (the earth being a part of the sun in the heavens, had not yet separated), and their children were ever thinking amongst themselves what might be the difference between darkness (evil) and light (good).*

After close examination of both passages, one is certainly inclined to believe that the primitive Polynesians, or the survivors of the lost continent Mu in the Pacific, got their belief and impressions through a much more ancient source of information than the people who recorded the story of the Bible, being thus but a repetition gathered from so-called "mythology." The mystery concerning such an origin of knowledge now classified as mythology, defying time itself, must have been of a truly divine character, taking into consideration the sinking of Atlantis and Mu, a submerging of continents where such knowledge was common in regard to fair gods that came from heaven and mixed with earthlings. Such a union alone is responsible and could in all likelihood account for the superior wisdom inbred into men at that time, enabling them to have a civilization all their own, at a time when the man of Europe was still a cave dweller, fearful and ever superstitious of elementary forces. A civilization here on this planet that may have easily been a true replica of the one known to the sons of God as the planet they inhabited, prior to the time of their descent upon earth and their union with earth females. The story of the Biblical flood coincides with the ancient records of the submersion of Atlantis and Mu; yet somehow there exists a strong suspicion that not all of mankind was eliminated by the flood, as the story in the Bible purports to show. Or else how can one explain the presence of the Australian bushman, the man in inner Africa, the Indian of all the Americas, the man of China and Tibet? Geographically, these people are separated by vast continents and oceans; yet somehow all of them have retained certain similar modes of life and customs from a remote past. Their bows and arrows, their feathers for decoration, war paint, braiding of hair, their music and dances — all point to a common origin of man prior to the flood and its separation of the survivors. If one wishes to accept the theory that man vanished after the great deluge, then where did the Mayan, Aztec, and Inca empires, which had their rise and decline after the sinking of Atlantis, come from?

All original earthlings, no matter where they are now located, had, with the exception of language, one important fact in common. They believed in the powers of Gods, in their invasions of earth, and their wars upon it, and in wars fought among the gods themselves. There is today hardly one tribe on this globe that does not have its own peculiar notion about the invaders that came from space and were accepted as gods and worshipped accordingly. How else can one explain all the totem poles in existence today all over the earth. Was it the constant fear in the minds of our ancestors all over the world that caused them to erect hideous and often gigantic totems in the hope of frightening off evil spirits, avenging gods, or demons which came from

## The Children of "Heaven and Earth"     119

space? Knowledge of these beings is so ancient and so interwoven with religions and dogmas that they are now regarded as myths; yet people all over the earth will tell you that the gods were fair—meaning white—that they came from heaven, and that man shall some day make it possible to go to heaven in space ships. The teaching that man shall inherit the universe, or rather expand his horizon by way of exploration within space, thus bringing the seed of man to all the planets suitable for life, is the humble admission of the God who said in Genesis 6:3 that they (the Gods) too are flesh — and therefore the union of the sons of God with earthlings serves but one main purpose — to create a super race from earth stock, in the hope that, with the proper tutoring, they too may learn to master the secrets of space travel and spread out in legions over the universe. If we substitute the word universal, which originally stood for the now common word catholic, then we well understand that the aim of the early church and its priests was to educate man to be universe conscious and to prepare him for expansion over that universe. Somehow, just the opposite did happen, and man is kept earthbound, shackled by those who prefer the gold of earth to the glory of the heavens or space. The teaching of the one who fully understood the meaning of the Father's house and its many mansions, or the Father's universe with its planets, has been shelved for the time being, by evil men, in order to keep man ignorant and within the boundaries of earth — in order to keep him here for their own foolish schemes, for their wars and miseries. The union of gods and men on this planet is, however, not heading for failure, but the fact that the original sons of God were in the minority, and earthmen in the majority, accounts for a temporary setback in spreading divine knowledge. That is one reason why we have so few men of God and so many men of the world. Only on rare occasions does a new leader, a messiah, an avatar, arrive on earth — a leader in whom is found truth, a prophet who does miracles and carries the God spark — so that man may be reminded of his heritage, become universe conscious, and recapture the old glory of being true children of heaven and earth, thus sons of God, reborn. For man's destiny lies not on earth — which is but the incubator for a super race of men; he was not meant to remain earthbound forever. "The works that I do, ye shall do also," includes the promise given to man that he shall duplicate a travel toward heaven, literally, and remain alive in doing so, that he shall live in the "Father's mansion."

*Ye shall wait but a little while, before ye shall see the glory of heavens (the worlds in space) prepared for you and ye shall suffer no more. For I have said it and my words are truth and they are life. Be ye comforted; I will show you the Father's house (universe) and more shall ye not want, for such as will believe there is no death, such servants will I show the Father.*

This and more the "King of truths" and master of arcane wisdom could have added to his words, for the benefit of man. Let us suppose he said them today, through the medium of his servants living in a modern age. Would it not be a blessing to know that the children of heaven and earth are quite as active and real as they were eons ago when they first bcame great men of renown, bringing with them the first semblance of civilization from another world?

## "SO BE IT UNTO YOU"

Who can say, beholding himself, Go now, for I know you not! Will he not be followed by himself unto the ends of earth forever? It is only a fool who will tell his shadow, Go, I know you not! Therefore, whether you created love or hatred within the sanctuary of your mind, so love or hatred will be your just reward, and none shall escape the fury and power of its materializing effects. Do not hide the mirror of your consciousness, reflecting the image of your Soul, expressing viewpoints, thoughts, desires. He that came did not conceal but reveal, giving mortals knowledge of the true man within man. He shall truly reign in all righteousness and glory, giving to all, not dividing and taking the riches within the depths of your imagination toward the fulfillment of dreams that are no longer dreams — for earth belongs to all earthlings — or how long can one steal from God that which is of God and not become a thief, robbing his own house?

Have great comfort, for men in their wickedness cannot harm you with idle chatter. He who disbelieves cannot disentangle himself from his own material thought web, but he will surely strangle his own Soul, destroying himself. Man's actions cannot hurt you, for ye that wear the garment of faith shall not see death but life. For when the desolation on earth (Atomic Warfare) and the confusion among men shall reach flood stages, know that you will stand with the high Lord, watching the avalanche of devastation roll by.

Hope is eternally young, and earthlings will not vanish for the sake of chosen ones that were before the earth began and shall be after the earth is old with age, for Spirit had its being in all for a time, and it lives unto eternity. Life abundant is not that which money can buy, or else the rich would have it. Neither does it belong to one or the other of the mighty ones of earth, or they would have it. Or do the modern sorcerers of earth believe that they alone possess the magic life abundant formula? Perhaps these ultra Thought wizards, selling heaven for a price, can also offer life abundant for a fraction of the golden calf unto you, by corralling men into weird-sounding organizations, telling their members that they have it, too.

Life abundant is the servant of such and master of none who accepts the mysteries of the mind, the "so be it unto you" which spells life abundant in our time, a gift, a blessing, the answer to prayer to him who has his genesis within the realm of Thought, seeking for divine, cosmic and arcane knowledge which comes to him who in the sacred silence had a glimpse of the infinite, seen with the eyes of man, spreading the glory of hope on earth, like a seed patiently awaiting the harvest within its limit of time.

> *Speak the Truth, give not away to Anger,*
> *Give of your little to him that asks of you;*
> *By these three things*
> *Men go to the realm of the Gods.*
>        THE DHAMMAPADA.

## SAYINGS OF RED LAMA

*Organizer and President of the American Budhist Society and Fellowship*

The fundamental Tenets and Dogmas of Budhistic Philosophy are incorporated within the "Sayings of RED LAMA."

"In this era of the Lord Maitreya — may truth and justice reign supreme."

"Prepare unlike the caterpillar for thy enchanted, sacred heritage. Realize that you have been and that in time you shall be again. Therefore, strive here for perfection, so that thy Heavenly Father grants you transfiguration."

"Red Lama came to splice together the existing loose ends of such as are of the truth, universally expressed by inspired men everywhere and so to establish a binding cord, harmonious in its combination, strong in spiritual union, colorful as the brilliance of prismatic reality, a pattern befitting, benevolent and beneficial for all mankind and the ages in which they shall have being."

"Let no man call me a master —for I am servant unto all — yet am I free, belonging to no one."

"To become a Budhist and to live as a Budhist, one has to be in love with truth. There are no other conditions so vital as this seeking and embracing of the principle which gives off the truth radiation. This must be experienced, before it can be understood."

"It is by asking questions, that enlightenment — which is the primal condition preceding Budhahood, comes to the individual. The most urgent need for people living today is to re-examine first themselves, thus beginning at the root whereby all things are conditioned for change, be it health, which is the first source of wealth, or material wealth."

"Budhism is not a religion, but a philosophy. Budhism as such respects all religious viewpoints and reflects upon their merits and demerits. Catholics are linked with the Budhists of Tibet and the East. Much was incorporated into the Catholic or Universal Church from the philosophy of the east. Yet what do we behold after nearly 2000 years of continuous preaching of the gospel of a man, which the religious leaders of his time murdered for the truth which was in him. Today there are about 800 million Budhists in the world, compared with the 300 million Christians, who in an endless repetition have their useless wars over fractions of opinions concerning the uplift of man. The Budhists of China and those of India did not war on one another for a thousand years. How is this for comparison of good will and peace toward men? The first commandment of the Budhists happens to be: "Thou shalt not kill anything." This good law was also adopted by the Christians — at least in part, but that is as far as it went. Which brings to my mind a certain story, with which you are no doubt all familiar. I shall however show you the same story in a different light — There has always existed a mystical bond and a reason for the fact, that the three holy men, the learned Magi left their mark of distinction with the Infant Jesus, thus shaping his destiny when still a child. The visit of the Magi overshadows with the philosophy and teaching of the East and Far East the very life and death of the Infant and Man Jesus. The gift of truth, the Budhi-Dhamma, the one not mentioned in the Bible —became indeed the most powerful gift of the Magi, left with the Child and His parents, enabling Jesus to attain — Christhood. Is it not rather strange, that in the Christian Cathedral of Cologne (my home town) are kept certain relics of the "Three Men from the East," who were Budhist. In the sacristy, crowned with 5000 gems are kept the sculls of the Magi named Caspar, Melchior and Balthazar, who worshipped at the cradle of Jesus the Child. The keeping of sculls for reverence is a typical Tibetan custom. Here is indeed food for thought —"

"The lama's are not magicians, neither are they or the Budhists idol worshippers, just because jealous and fanatical religionists say so? Visible and material images important for reference, are doors, through which by meditation invisible and spiritual force issues forth good or evil, thus entering the world of mortals. So if the Budhist has his patrons upon which he meditates for divine aid, was this not also adopted by the Christians of our time, calling them saints."

"Come along the road with us. Thus shall we bear with your questions in regard of the philosophy of the East."

"Seek ye for divine blessings at each full of the

moon, when spiritual communion or Shambalah can be established through meditation."

"The great ones see, whereas the average person remains negative to spiritual truths. We all have the God-given right to change our minds if by doing so, it puts one's Soul at ease."

"If you are of the truth, it will not be hard to absorb same. This is the aim of all Budhists."

"By living a decent and useful life, Budhists believe to eliminate an endless chain of reincarnations — thus becoming free spiritual agents for good."

"Such as are in "love with truth" are Budhists — even if they never heard the word before."

"Truth is a sword, keen-edged and pointy. He who wields same is liable to run into opposition. If one however feels saturated with the force of truth, one fears not the forces of evil and fights regardless of odds."

"Truth and prophesy will become a gift to such as are in tune with nature, displayed in so many various ways to us humans."

"He that seeketh, is entitled to all he findeth — be the values material or spiritual."

"Seek ye first a pleasing house for Spirit to dwell therein. All the other things shall in time materialize. My symbol, the triangle mounted up on a square is called Dju Kung in Tibetan, or Spirit house. You can clean house by beginning with yourself and thus erect your own Dju Kung — if you but will."

"Not all have to go to Tibet, in order to find the door to the inner mysteries. Some of us find this door sooner than others. Indeed each of us is a high priest of his own temple — his living body. Using meditation as a key, telepsychism and one's astral body, it should not be too hard to learn and listen to such, not meant for everybody's benefit. Those things I know and I believe them to be true, wishing to learn more, as I walk the earth, Spirit disguised as man, labled with a name given when I issued forth from the womb of a woman. The divine and universal creator is chiefly interested in "living temples" for he is the God of the living, admonishing man: "Turn yourselves and live ye" — Ezekiel 18:32. Erect therefore your own Dju Kung."

"Is not the past like a mirror and as such reflects deeds done — good or evil — upon the time river ... You cannot fail to recognize your image in your own time, when looking deep into this river. With it comes understanding — you know then, that you are but a part of its current, which surely carries its own to an all embracing, endless pool of all-knowledge, all-spirit, all-peace."

My brief impressions on Nirvana without borrowing and practising Yoga:

Nirvana is absence of tension, both mentally and physically — a "letting-yourself-go," a sinking into fathomless, but blessful forgetfulness. Nirvana is Soul submersion of all conscious thought — a brief spell of being at one with universal, vibratory laws, a seeking to attune oneself with all living substance, unlimited throughout space and beyond this planet. The East knows such blessed moments as nirvana, without monopoly and restrictions thereupon. Nirvana depends entirely on one's power of free will with an ultimate effect upon one's well being and this is the priceless gem worn by the conscious Soul at all times, under all conditions and in the sight of men.

OM MANI PADME HUM
Oh, Thou Jewel in the Lotus

## THE MYSTIC TALISMAN

PROTECT US LORD from things unseen,
From things unwholesome and unclean,
From floating phantoms in the night,
From Evil forces shining bright,
From seeing things that are not there,
From drifting specters in the air,
From dreams that turn your blood to ice,
From terror in the dark precise,
From shadows whispering of death,
From unseen hands that strangle you in bed,
From cunning witchcraft poisoning ones head,
From walking creatures that are dead,
From strangers not of three dimensions,
From things beyond earthly comprehension,
From things we do not knowing why,
From the influence of the Evil eye,
From sounds no human can endure,
From poisons that will kill you sure,
From creatures that are Evil incarnate,
From humans possessed by spirits but of hate,
From spells cast by a black magician,
From sorcery that will deliver you to a mortician,
From those who wish to steal your mind,
From such that never say a word that's kind,
From those that live as vampires do,
From drinking of demonly brew,
From all such things that leave the mind quite mad,
From such that kill all joy and leave you sad,
From forces that have never been divine,
From all such that will turn you into swine,
From such and more too numerous to mention,
PROTECT US LORD from ever having bad intentions.

AMON, AMEN, — OM MANI PADME HUM

Printed in the United States
94424LV00006B/68/A